A COURSE IN MIRACLES –
A GIFT FOR ALL MANKIND

A
COURSE
IN MIRACLES
A GIFT
For All Mankind

—————— Second Edition ——————

Tara Singh

Ballantine Books • New York

Copyright © 1986, 1992 by Tara Singh

All rights reserved under International and Pan-American Copyright Conventions. No part of this book may be used or reproduced in any manner without written permission except in the case of brief quotations embodied in critical articles and reviews. For information, address Life Action Press, P.O. Box 48932, Los Angeles, California 90048. Published in the United States by Ballantine Books, a division of Random House, Inc., New York, and distributed in Canada by Random House of Canada Limited, Toronto. This edition published by arrangement with Foundation for Life Action, Inc.

Portions from *A Course in Miracles* © 1975 and *The Gifts of God* © 1982 Reprinted by permission of the Foundation for Inner Peace, Inc., P.O. Box 1104, Glen Ellen, California 95442.

Library of Congress Catalog Card Number: 93-90043

ISBN: 0-345-38404-0

Cover design by Susan Lovelace
Art by Dr. Cleo Dixon

Manufactured in the United States of America

First Ballantine Books Edition: October 1992

10 9 8 7 6 5 4 3 2 1

ACKNOWLEDGMENTS

I am most grateful for the goodness and assistance of the following friends in preparing *A Course in Miracles – A Gift for All Mankind:* Barbara Dunlap, Aliana Scurlock, Jim Cheatham, Charles Johnson, Frank Nader, Bette Schneider, Lucille Frappier, Johanna Macdonald, Jim Walters, and Norah Ryan.

CONTENTS

FOREWORD

A Course in Miracles is a cultural and publishing phenomenon. Since its publication in 1976, nearly 1,000,000 copies have been sold. Without advertising or the backing of a major publisher, the *Course* has found its growing audience largely through word-of-mouth.

In this revised and expanded edition of *A Gift for All Mankind*, Tara Singh brings *A Course in Miracles* into sharp focus as the first scripture to offer a step-by-step curriculum for undoing the patterns of thought which keep us separated from God, ourselves, and each other.

Why does the nightmare of personal unfulfillment and social conflict continue? Has affluence helped? Education? Religion? Why not? People want answers. But we can't think our way out of our problems. In *A Gift for All Mankind*, Tara Singh underscores the revolutionary premise of the *Course:*

> "The very means by which we think is corrupt. And, within that corrupt framework, we want to have better thoughts. But 'thoughts' cannot *be* better."

A three-part volume originally published in English (then translated into Spanish and soon to be offered in

Portuguese and German), *A Course in Miracles* challenges us to transform the way we perceive everything and everyone including ourselves. Yet the *Course* is not a program for self-improvement. Rather it helps us undo everything that blinds us to our own perfection.

The Introduction to *A Course in Miracles* says, *"The course does not aim at teaching the meaning of love, for that is beyond what can be taught. It does aim, however, at removing the blocks to the awareness of love's presence...."* The *Text* adds, *"Knowledge is not the motivation for learning this course. Peace is."* *

Does the *Course* work? Like all timeless wisdom, its words are easy to learn, more difficult to apply.

Tara Singh was told directly by the Scribe of the *Course,* Dr. Helen Schucman, *"A Course in Miracles* is to be lived, not to be learned." Tara Singh's approach to reading the *Course* is consistent with this instruction.

A Course in Miracles is comprised of a *Text,* a *Workbook for Students,* and a *Manual for Teachers.* The *Workbook* includes 365 lessons – one for each day of the year.

In Part I of *A Gift for All Mankind,* Tara Singh offers an introduction to the *Course* that is both demanding and richly rewarding. With compelling insight into the pressures of personal life and our society's moral contradictions, he offers ways to simplify our life style and find the inner strength to meet any challenge.

---

* *A Course in Miracles, Text,* page 128. [Second Edition: T-8. I. 1:1-2. page 138.]

Part II explores the first ten lessons of the *Course*. Here Tara Singh demonstrates the wholehearted attention required to receive its gifts: new energy, clarity, and conviction.

When Tara Singh first encountered *A Course in Miracles* in 1976, he had already come to the silent mind necessary to receive truth. Thus, his commentaries on the *Course* carry the power of realized words.

One person's transformation would be a gift for all mankind. Tara Singh's book shows why *A Course in Miracles* makes it possible.

Editor

PREFACE

The impact of one encounter
has the power to bring us to holy relationship
with everyone in the world,
because Life is One and Love, indivisible.
A single meeting of Andrew, John, and Peter with Jesus
transformed their lives for all time
by introducing them to eternity.
A Teacher of God
does not acknowledge separation as real
but only as a mistake which can be corrected.

My very first encounter
with *A Course in Miracles* [1]
brought me into direct contact with the vitality
inherent in the Thoughts of God in the *Course*.
The only reality is the Will of God
which eternally extends itself.
Time is the only illusion.

The pure energy of the Thoughts of God
makes application of the daily lesson
of *A Course in Miracles* possible.
Every single sentence
is endowed with a miracle
to undo the illusion of time.
The Holy Spirit awakens us
from the belief in separation
and accompanies us all through the day.

> As the teacher of God advances in his train-
> ing, he learns one lesson with increasing
> thoroughness. He does not make his own
> decisions; he asks his Teacher for His
> answer, and it is this he follows as his guide
> for action. [2]

Almost all scriptures are written
by people inspired by Incarnations of God.
But *A Course in Miracles*
offers the Thoughts of God directly.
It is not a religion.
Its purpose is to help the individual find inner peace.

> *This is a course in how to know yourself.* [3]

> *To your most holy Self all praise is due for
> what you are, and for what He is Who created
> you as what you are.* [4]

In an age where

> *My meaningless thoughts are showing me
> a meaningless world,* [5]

a sense of helplessness surrounds us.
Pressured by time and problems,
we are ruled by insecurity and unfulfillment.
Having already lost our work
we are now subject to jobs.
Thus we are false to ourselves.
Imperceptibly, people everywhere
are reduced to being mercenaries.
Living by choices,

they have lost the discrimination and wisdom
to make their own decisions.

Wisdom is one's own; it is direct,
not externally influenced.
Its clarity is what it would take
to see a fact as a fact.

But *A Course in Miracles* comes to awaken us
from man-made illusion
to the God-created Self, which realizes

     I am not the victim of the world I see. [6]

Students who make contact
with the energy of the *Course*
give integrity to everything they do.
They start by bringing order in their lives.
They live by

     I will not value what is valueless. [7]

The *Course* insists that we dissolve
every contradiction and conflict instantly.
This means undoing opinions
and judgments with their consequences
in order to come to holy relationship.
Thus the Holy Spirit teaches
the consistency of moving from fact to fact
until one ends separation
and comes to the Action of Life itself.

*   *   *

When I first encountered the *Course*,
I came to a decision to give myself fully
to discovering the truth of its daily lesson.
It led me from understanding the *Course*
intellectually
to making it real: a recognition of being,
untouched by words.
Intellectual understanding is of mere ideas.
A Course in Miracles is to be lived.
Realization is your discovery
that the Thoughts of God are true.
Recognition restores the awareness
of your own magnitude and wholeness.

I discovered

> *The curriculum is highly individualized, and all aspects are under the Holy Spirit's particular care and guidance. Ask and He will answer. The responsibility is His, and He alone is fit to assume it.*

> *To do so is His function.*
> *To refer the questions to Him is yours.* [8]

> *Prepare for this each morning, remember God when you can throughout the day, ask the Holy Spirit's help when it is feasible to do so, and thank Him for His guidance at night.* [9]

As the *Course* points out,
the function of the Son of God – each one of us –
is *to share.*

I had resistance to teaching
because it was my conviction
that one should not interfere in the life of another
unless one knows the truth.
But I was made aware of the Eternal Laws
of the teaching-learning relationship
in the *Manual for Teachers:*

> *The course... emphasizes that to teach* is *to
> learn.... It also emphasizes that teaching is a
> constant process.* [10]

> *In the teaching-learning situation, each one
> learns that giving and receiving are the same.* [11]

Therefore, I realized that
the Name of God cannot be commercialized.
How can the Given be sold?
Obviously, love energizes itself by sharing.

Love is not of past or future.
What is of the living moment is the sharing of

> *... everlasting holiness and peace.* [12]

One-to-one relationship
leads to meeting in the Oneness of Life
where separation ends.

In 1983, the One Year Non-Commercialized Retreat:
A Serious Study of *A Course in Miracles* began
with students from all over the country.
Bringing *A Course in Miracles* into application
changed our life style and values.
We discovered the need
to be independent of the externals through

self-reliance,
intrinsic work, and
having something of our own to give.

Freed from a sense of lack,
a small group of men and women
stepped out of jobs
in order to live a productive life.

Do you realize what is involved
in coming to self-reliance?
Who would work with a small group
and give himself to a non-commercialized life?
Would his not have to be an action
born of fulfillment?

Without the vitality of gratefulness
no one can overcome the self-centered outlook
of commercial life.
You and I would have to be related
to the given strength of the One
... in charge of the process of Atonement. [13]
In the *Text,* the Author of *A Course in Miracles,*
the Son of God, speaks in the first person:

*I am in charge of the process of Atonement,
which I undertook to begin. When you offer a
miracle to any of my brothers, you do it to
yourself and me.... My part in the Atonement
is the canceling out of all errors that you
could not otherwise correct. When you have
been restored to the recognition of your
original state, you naturally become part of
the Atonement yourself. As you share my
unwillingness to accept error in yourself and
others, you must join the great crusade to
correct it; listen to my voice, learn to undo
error and act to correct it.* [14]

We have completed ten years
of one-to-one relationship
under the auspices of the Foundation for Life Action,
a federally recognized, nonprofit
educational foundation.

From intensive study of the curriculum
of *A Course in Miracles*
emerged a school
– "Having the Ears to Hear" –
situated at *The Branching of the Road*.[15]
The school deals with the individual's
INHERENT UNWILLINGNESS
to change from passive to co-creative energies.
Its curriculum is consistent
with *A Course in Miracles*.
It is for the serious student
whose first love is God,
for whom nothing short of ending separation
is acceptable.

The school is not for those who want to be students
but for those who are already students and

"... have the ears to hear." [16]

The *Text* states:

> *When you come to the place where the branch
> in the road is quite apparent, you cannot go
> ahead. You must go either one way or the
> other.... The whole purpose of coming this
> far was to decide which branch you will take
> now. The way you came no longer matters. It
> can no longer serve. No one who reaches this
> far can make the wrong decision, although he
> can delay.* [17]

The Foundation for Life Action
is a school for training teachers
to bring *A Course in Miracles* into application
so they may be part of God's plan for salvation. [18]
It provides an atmosphere
in which to live a life style
consistent with the Path of Virtue. [19]
We do not seek donations or ask for charity;
nor do we have a community or own property.

In order for the student
to overcome insecurity and self-centeredness,
and be independent of the externals, we undertake

    – not to work for another
    – to discover our own intrinsic work
    – to be self-reliant

– to have something of our own to give
– to lead a non-commercialized life
– and not to take advantage of another.

The teachers of God have trust in the world, because they have learned that it is not governed by the laws the world made up. It is governed by a Power That is in them but not of them. It is this Power That keeps all things safe. It is through this Power that the teachers of God look on a forgiven world. [20]

For us the fact is:

I do not perceive my own best interests....
What I think are my best interests
would merely bind me closer
to the world of illusions. [21]

Only God's plan for salvation will work. [22]

My only function is the one God gave me. [23]

A happy outcome to all things is sure. [24]

No one can fail who seeks to reach the truth. [25]

*   *   *

A Course in Miracles – A Gift for All Mankind is drawn from sharings which have taken place since the beginning of the One Year Non-Commercialized Retreat.

Tara Singh

INTRODUCTION

I often feel that without *A Course in Miracles* my life would have been empty. One such gift makes life meaningful. Who brought it? How did it ever come to the earth plane? It fills one with wonder.

Why was *A Course in Miracles* given when there are already so many religions and scriptures in the world? All scriptures are holy, regardless of their religious origin. The words of the Hebrew prophets are true; the words of great Chinese sages are absolute; the words of Indian saints are eternal and true. So also, the words of Islam in the Koran are of God. Why, then, another book?

Why did *A Course in Miracles* come today? Why in our generation? Why in English? Why were we deprived of it for twenty centuries, fifty centuries?

What answers would you give to these questions? Answers born out of relative knowledge are not answers at all. We are so educated. We know so much that it is very difficult to receive a truth. Our very knowing has become detrimental.

If you are sensitive and sincere, you must feel the pain of not knowing reality, of not knowing love or truth directly. Do you ever feel that? Have you ever yearned for truth? If you have, you won't settle for the false.

PART I

CHAPTER ONE

1

Why *A Course in Miracles?*

To see what brought *A Course in Miracles* into being, we have to look at what necessitated it. The *Course* is not something whimsical that somebody just wrote. It is a gift of God to His Son.

There is an Eternal Law that a need must be met. Somewhere, deep within each one of us, there must have been a tremendous cry for something beyond what was already in the scriptures – for something direct, something that could be understood. Most of the scriptures of the world have been translated and interpreted. And when interpretation takes place, thought (or relative knowledge) interferes with it.

And yet there is a yearning in each one of us to know God, to know truth, to know peace, to know love – everything that is inaccessible to the conscious mind. We substitute attachment for love, opinion and belief for truth, pleasure for joy. And very few of us have gone beyond these substitutes. We think that we love, that we know truth. We are convinced of the reality of our opinions and our feelings, even of our limitations.

Beyond our opinions and feelings, however, we yearn to know what is real, to know the timelessness of our being. Before Moses, Buddha, Jesus, and Mohammed – throughout the ages – this yearning spurred us on.

Our yearning began when we separated ourselves from God. Separation is the only state we've known. It is the source of our drive for wholeness and holiness. If we are whole, all is resolved. Separation always longs for peace, for wholeness, for contentment. As long as separation is there, yearning is there.

In fact, the yearning within each of us brought about *A Course in Miracles*.

There is no other scripture like it. It is in English, the most evolved English you will find anywhere. By that I mean it is precise. It defines every word. And it does not use one single word that is not a fact. It doesn't preach; it just presents the fact.

A Course in Miracles relates to us directly. It deals with the issues we have to face within ourselves. Throughout the centuries, we have consistently avoided them.

In dealing with basic issues, the *Course* challenges you to undo the past. When you have undone the past in your consciousness, you are a light unto yourself. In the present, you are true to yourself and can receive the Absolute. Then you are free from all your "knowing." This state can be called religious.

We need to understand what the human brain is and what it does. The human brain is physical. It functions like a computer. It records all that has happened to you, all you have experienced and learned. It is a storehouse. It knows only what has been put into it, and so you are limited to what you have known. That is the human brain. As a matter of fact, the human being is now a second-rate computer, reduced to nothing but jobs. It is tragic.

Can you come to an intense awareness that you want to be out of this mess of "knowing" and prejudice? Do you want to come alive, be reborn and resurrected? Do you want to know the Absolute – not opinion, but the Absolute? Love is Absolute. The brain can't know it, and the computer can't know it. But *A Course in Miracles* makes it accessible – the direct Word of God.

Whatever anyone has said in the past is not necessarily your truth. When Jesus said, "I and my Father are one," [1] it was His truth at that time, not yours when you say it. If you say, "I and my Father are one," isn't it a lie? Isn't it just words, limited to the brain?

As an individual, you have a responsibility to be wise and perceptive. You are a child of God, a creation of clarity. Don't ever underestimate your potential. Systems have always fallen apart, whether it's the Roman or the Greek or the British. Napoleons have come and gone, as have the Hitlers and the czars. They don't last; but the human being does.

The wise person never loses confidence in the human being. And he never trusts a system, regardless of its name. In the end, they are all corrupt. That is the effect of time on things – degeneration. Even if something is noble at the outset, in time it will start deteriorating. Everywhere it is the same.

To give importance to systems, to dogmas, and to ideologies is to ignore your own intrinsic worth. You are more valuable than these. You are eternal and they are not. When people deceive each other into believing in a system, you can see the beginning of the end of that system. An undeceived person knows this. When Ralph Waldo Emerson saw the locomotive at the age of nineteen, he said that the seeds of destruction were inherent in this progress. Are we capable of heeding, or will we continue promoting our so-called progress?

Lincoln also warned us. He said that prosperity breeds tyrants. If we could hear this, it would revolutionize our lives. We have to find wisdom to free ourselves from the mess we are in.

Today we worship helplessness though there is nothing religious about it. Tell me, who is not helpless and dependent upon someone else? Where there is dependence, there is no relationship. Relationship is at the level of Life itself, not at the level of concepts and ideas.

Where is our individuality? To be an individual we have to be free of fear. But we are all ruled by fear, insecurity, anger, greed, and jealousy. We have but one brain, and we are all subject to its conditioning. Fear is not Chinese, nor is anger Indian, nor is insecurity American. When we are afraid, we all behave the same way. We have been deceived. We need a different outlook on life. It's time to wake up! But can we afford to? It requires wisdom.

Wisdom is rare. It takes guts. It demands a sense of dignity, responsibility. Wisdom does not react. But wisdom can say, "No." Wisdom is your own love, an awakening which flowers in you. When you are wise you know that you are holy. And the holy do not scare the world. They don't organize anything or promote a belief system. They are humane, and their light cannot be hidden. What they do is ever new. It is an extension of the Source of Life.

When you are not related to Life, then you are isolated. You need a job to support yourself and all kinds of outlets – beer, cigarettes, television, magazines – just so that you don't have to face yourself.

Over the centuries we thought that if we were not poor, then we would be happy. Yet, in this age of affluence, we have more psychosomatic diseases, more rapes, more murders, and more suicides than ever before. What has happened to our marriages? Why do our children no longer have reverence for their parents? How can we continue to believe in our illusions?

We thought if we were educated, that would improve our lot: maybe the whole misery of life stemmed from lack of schooling. So we tried education. But still there is no wisdom. We became affluent, but no wiser. Education and affluence only encouraged further deterioration. Can you see that? More wars, more hate, more propaganda, more restlessness, more distractions. Distractions. Distractions. Distractions.

Life has become a burden. We work like a machine for somebody else, reduced to nothing but a life of habit and routine. And we are planning, full blast, head-on, universal destruction. That's a fact. Education without wisdom is self-destructive.

There is a man-made world and a God-created world. We live in the man-made world. Whether you are a philosopher or a peasant, it takes wisdom to know the God-created world. When you're related with it, you harness its energy and wisdom. You also know your own dignity, your own sacredness. Now we know only skills, insecurity, and the fear of losing our jobs.

Then we thought, "Well, maybe religion will help." But the scriptures haven't helped either – neither the Torah, nor the Gita, nor the Bible. Because we thought by learning...well, tell me what have we learned? Can we learn wisdom? Can we learn to be free of fear?

We can read about Moses all we want, but we don't need Moses to come and part the sea again. We can read about Elijah or Daniel, we can read the Koran, we can read the Vedas, but our reading is merely an activity of the brain. We can memorize them; we can quote them; we can become professors or priests. But in the end, we'll be nothing but professionals.

Saints are not professionals. They are never in the shrines where people have been indoctrinated with one "ism" or another. How could they live in a world of fragmentation?

Could you be a saint and be a Christian? Could you be a saint and still be a Hindu? Could you be a saint and remain a Moslem? The saint is grateful that religion has served its purpose. He steps out of it; he becomes universal. Then he frees us from our prejudices and conflicts. He talks about wholeness because he has come to wholeness.

So, religions have not helped, affluence has not helped, education has not helped. And all the political dogmas have not helped either. We are more bound today than ever before.

Now, after centuries, a miracle has happened – a real miracle. And can you imagine, we can't even recognize a miracle anymore. We are fatigued by our routine. We are so educated that we've lost our innocence. We've lost silence and the knowledge of stillness within. Our "knowing" has become our bondage. It knows the names of stars, metals, trees, and animals, but it doesn't know reality, it doesn't know Life.

But the miracle did happen. *A Course in Miracles* came. It says neither learning, nor religion, nor affluence has worked. Why? Because learning must be brought into application – application is what is missing.

So politicians can speak *about* peace, while they are preparing for war. No one would nominate Lincoln today. He would refuse to trim his beard, polish his shoes, and wear the clothes that Madison Avenue dictates. A man like Lincoln would start undoing our illusions, wouldn't he? He would be uncompromising, a man of conviction with a voice of his own. And no one would listen to him.

We don't want to let go of our belief systems. This is true everywhere. I am not talking about a particular country or people, I'm talking about how the human being has been indoctrinated. Whether in Chile or China, wherever, unless you are part of the clan, you're in trouble. The masses just go along because they have no mind of their own.

To have a mind of your own, you have to have wisdom. Then you don't fit into the crowd. You have your own resources and what you do is new. Then you would appreciate *A Course in Miracles* because it starts with undoing; it doesn't promote anything. It tells us the truth as we would understand it.

Prophet after prophet came to the world. They did great things and we revered them. But *they* were the "holy ones," so to speak. The rest of us got lost in seeking gratification and security, caught in our prejudices and the activity of the physical senses.

A Course in Miracles gives *us* the keys to overcome the world. It has no symbolism. This is phenomenal. This was the next step that had to be taken. He Who overcame the world had to find ways to help us do the same. In *A Course in Miracles,* He holds us by the hand and leads us to freedom from the world.

We must have taken birth this time to be among the blessed generation that was to know the truth. Do we have the ears to hear? How we deprive ourselves when we lack gratefulness and discrimination.

For a long time hardly anyone recognized Jesus. To know the greatness of Jesus in His own time would have taken a tremendous sense of discrimination. To recognize the eternal demands wisdom and eyes that see.

A Course in Miracles was published anonymously. Someone gave us the *Course.* That someone rose to the *state* of the *Course,* surpassed the nameless names, and became One. Therefore, she never wrote her name on it, never said, "I did it."

It's very interesting that out of probably the most materialistic country in the world could emerge the greatest gift ever given to humanity. It defies all laws, all assumptions, all judgments. It's like Moses freeing the slaves, or Guru Nanak* lifting the untouchables from their misery. The *Course* liberates us from our materialistic mentality.

A Course in Miracles has come to the New World to bring it to new consciousness. And it helps us with application. It says never mind your belief system; whether you are Buddhist, Christian, or Hindu is of little importance. You can read the *Course* because miracles are independent of belief systems. A miracle is only the relationship of the body with that which is not of the body. The correction the miracle offers takes

---

* Guru Nanak (1469-1538 or 1539) was the prophet who founded the Sikh religion. Editor

place within you, not in the synagogue or in the church or in the temple. You are the temple of God, and that is where the transformation takes place.

So *A Course in Miracles* says that we don't have to be dependent on another person or another system. Awakening begins with you. And believe it or not, that's not what we really want. We want to focus on people out there. We'll do anything to avoid confronting ourselves.

Organized religions preach dogma. But have they brought about application, or merely spread their own belief systems? Belief systems are of the brain, of the earth. What is *not* of the earth is given to you when you are still and, therefore, part of God's Mind. Without stillness, you will never know what is eternal, what is real. There is less and less stillness in the world today, more haste and pressure.

*   *   *

There are two kinds of teachers. One promotes the preaching of dogma. He extends the belief system that supports him. He doesn't believe *I am sustained by the Love of God.* [2] He knows he is sustained by his church. So that's what he promotes. I could be very successful extending Hinduism. I could say nice things about karma and reincarnation, and you would think, "Christianity doesn't have that. This sounds great!"

The other teacher introduces you to the Mind of God, of which you are a part. To this enlightened being, nothing is external. He can look at the tree and see the eternal, purifying vitality of water and air. Being one with the Mind of God, which does not externalize, he sees the fallacy in which we are caught. And he tries to awaken us to truth saying, "Look, you are eternal." He doesn't say truth is Buddhist or Hindu. He just says you are *it*.

A Course in Miracles also says you are important. You are as much a part of the Mind of God as any prophet that ever lived. The only thing is that the prophet realized that truth. You see? And then he tried to share it with others, telling them, "You can do it." "You can do what I have done, and more." [3]

The world needs us to start extending wholeness, because that is what we are. Otherwise, we will extend some belief system – religious, political, or economic.

What are you extending? Confusion must project confusion. If you are confused, you're going to elect a confused president. Why do you participate in this mania? Why don't you find your own reality, your own resources?

Where do you think *A Course in Miracles* would start? Where would the Mind of God begin? The *Course* would have to start with undoing, questioning our deceptions. Undoing means unlearning, not more learning.

A Course in Miracles has nothing to sell; it is not a belief system. The *Course* is the Thoughts of God. When it says, *I am sustained by the Love of God,* that's the truth. When you *realize* the truth of it, only then can you say you know it. If you just know it intellectually, it doesn't do a thing. The responsibility to realize it is ours.

Why would the *Course* or a real teacher start that way? That's a wonderful question, isn't it? Why do the real teacher and *A Course in Miracles* start with undoing? Why do they insist that we look at our deceptions? Why? Because only the Real knows the truth that you are already perfect.

No one who has realized the truth that you are already perfect is going to sell perfection or what you have to do to get there. He's going to say, "Look, the layers and layers of conditioning that blind you to the light are what you have to remove." On the other hand, the one who sells belief systems knows nothing of the fact that the human being is perfect.

So how does the *Course* undo? The first lesson is *Nothing I see..means anything.* [4] That's quite a blow. You think you know what things mean; it says you don't. Unless you come to humility, you're in conflict.

The next lesson is *I have given everything I see..all the meaning that it has for me.* [5] And that's true, too. When I buy a car, I protect it, polish it, and call the police if I see you take it. I am giving it meaning. But ideas have no meaning. Just as the word "car" doesn't mean anything – it's a name given to a symbol – so are ideas abstract. The "knowing" of our man-made thought system is no knowing at all. Among ideas, we think some are good and some are bad; they are based on duality. The *Course* doesn't support duality. Duality is *our* conflict.

There is a story of two Zen monks. They were about to cross a stream when they saw a young woman who couldn't manage it. One of them put her on his back and carried her across. Later, the other one scolded him, "I can't understand. You are a monk! You're never to look at a woman. You're never to touch one. How could you do that?" The monk answered, "Well, I left her there. You are still carrying her."

A Course in Miracles brings us to the sanity that begins to question. By questioning our belief system, we can undo it. As the Thoughts of God, the *Course* can dissolve man-made thought. And when it does this, we are free.

The only freedom, as Thoreau said, is freedom from self. When you are responsible for yourself in the true sense, then you are free from your brain's activity and from "earth energy,"* with its aggression and instinct for survival.

When you are free, then you are at peace – in a state of stillness. You want nothing, for you are not of the earth, you are of the Kingdom of God. And you have nothing to preach. You introduce your brothers and sisters to eternity; and you don't charge for it because you have overcome insecurity. You are not part of the

---

* For a detailed exploration into "earth energies," see "Why Has There Always Been War in the World?" in *The Future of Mankind: Affluence without Wisdom Is Self-Destructive* by Tara Singh, Life Action Press, 1992. Editor

survival system that leads to greed, cleverness, and a routine life.

You are a free person, full of gratefulness for the glory of creation. In its joy of being, even the earth creates the most beautiful flowers. Everything sings the glory of God in creation, never wanting to be anything other than what it is. A tree is a tree, a fruit is a fruit. There is perfection in the orange seed that can again produce endless oranges. And who knows the reality of the color orange? If you knew what a color was, you could be healed just by looking at the color itself.

We look at the world with sightless eyes because we are preoccupied with the brain and thought. It's time that we opened our eyes. When the mind is still, you see the miracle that the tree is, the miracle that the child is – you see perfection in everything.

The manifest world can relate you to perfection, if you see it with stillness. The purpose of everything manifested is to relate you with its Source. The Source is eternal, all-encompassing. Without the sun, the soil, the air, the water, or the moon, the flower could not grow. The flower relates you to everything in existence. The brain separates everything from wholeness and fragments it. The action of God's Thought is to restore it to wholeness.

The approach of *A Course in Miracles* is compassionate. The *Course* points out that even if you don't understand or believe it, it's quite all right. Just do the simple exercises and don't make a problem of it. As you go along, you begin to see that you are changing involuntarily because of these simple lessons. There is more to them than we realize.

After we have done the first ten lessons in the *Course,* we see some of them repeated in a slightly different form. It is like a spiral. Each time a similar lesson appears, we seem to understand it better. It makes a lot more sense than when we first saw it.

These thoughts do not mean anything [6] appears the second time as *My thoughts do not mean anything.* [7] If you could honestly say *My thoughts do not mean anything,* you would be enlightened.

We say all kinds of things we don't mean. What is true has to be lived. Understanding is not enough. We can understand a great deal. In fact, our problem today is not that we don't know enough, but that we know too much. Yet our understanding is not always complete. There is a tremendous gap between understanding and application. It takes wholeheartedness to bridge that gap.

Most of the world's religions inspire us to live consistent with Divine Laws or with the path of virtue. We are urged to love our neighbor, be truthful, know ourselves, and so forth. *A Course in Miracles* doesn't leave it at that, because we can repeat the words and still not live them. The *Course* emphasizes that they have to be lived. Application is essential.

Lesson 48 says, *There is nothing to fear.* [8] Do we meet the challenge of this statement and live by it? We can read and try to understand it, but if fear is still there, we have not been transformed by the truth of these words.

One way or another, we justify not bringing the lesson to application. We say we are tired, we'll do it when the circumstances are right – all kinds of things. Very few of us can truthfully say, *There is nothing to fear,* or say anything that we really mean. Isn't it alarming that we say things we don't mean?

I am sustained by the Love of God.[9] If you could say this and mean it, and not just intellectually understand it, you would have no room for insecurity in your life. This truth would alter your values and relationship with everything.

The wisdom of the *Course* is that it begins with the undoing of our "knowing" that knows no reality. Thought does not relate man to reality, yet we give it authority over us.

Christianity, like Buddhism, Hinduism and other religions, states that THOU SHALT NOT KILL.[10] If we lived by this principle, would there be wars in the world? The clergy on all sides have overlooked this. Verbal agreement has no meaning, but we are quite comfortable with our inconsistencies.

The *Course* doesn't teach, if you look very keenly at it. What does one teach but ideas and concepts? Of course, you can teach a skill, like sailing a boat, but we are talking about Reality. It is another matter to undo the psychological fears that we project and the concepts that lead us to clash with one another. If conflict continues within us, then we have war and discord – the reflection of that conflict within.

The *Course* doesn't promote dependence. It introduces you to self-sufficiency. The teachings that say "I know and you don't," or the priest knows and the layman doesn't, or some politician knows and you don't – these are to be questioned. If none of us is at peace within, we all meet at the same level.

The person at peace is not ambitious. What would he be like? What is his function in society? One thing is sure, he would quickly be put in jail. Or he would not get a visa to enter the country. Jesus would have a tough time. He would remind us that we say "In God We Trust." [11] Who trusts in God? And yet for a century, we have bandied around that phrase.

*　　*　　*

There are two things in this world we can't afford: silence and innocence. We have too much to do; we are so wound up. Silence brings us to innocence. And the function of *A Course in Miracles* is to bring us to that silence.

Every sentence of the *Course* brings illusions to truth and dissolves them. And a miracle takes place. To come to that state where the miracle takes place, we will have to totally change our approach to reading.

Very few people in the world know how to read. Reading means silencing the mind, not accumulating knowledge. We don't have the right relationship with the *Course* if we are accumulating more ideas, more beliefs, more knowledge. Each sentence of the daily lesson must bring you to silence. Then by the end, you are in a different space. There is a vitality within you that you've never felt before. This is the vitality of silence – the strongest experience you can ever have.

Silence is not touched by words. It is a state where contradictions end and a renewal takes place. There is nothing mysterious about it. It has no means, no techniques, no secrets or mantras. For any method activates thought. Whatever busies the mind contradicts innocence and silence and dissipates energy.

Every lesson's gift of silence and space brings you to wholeness. You directly experience it. This direct experience changes the quality of your reading. Then when you read *I am sustained by the Love of God,* you would insist that these words be true for you.

We think we can live in the world without integrity or conviction. But the conflict between the way we live and our ideals torments us. As long as this conflict continues, the need for outlets is inevitable. Life becomes more and more artificial.

And today we face the prospect of mass unemployment. To the industrial economy, the human being is not important – nuclear submarines are. We don't have the money to feed starving people, but we have plenty of money for weapons. This is the opposite of love.

As you read the *Course,* you begin to see that life is sustained by Eternal Laws. For millennia the earth has been supported by the sun, the moon, the rain, and the balance of the elements. It has its own vitality, rhythm, and beauty because life is consistent with Eternal Laws. Everything is related.

Life is One.

Because of our separation and isolation, we create conflict within which exploits the earth and our neighbors. All over the world the rich are getting richer, and our value system is becoming more and more corrupt.

* * *

A Course in Miracles begins to relate you with your eternity. The *Course* doesn't teach or preach because it stands on the premise that you are already perfect. Don't you have difficulty believing this? You have already concluded otherwise about yourself. *A Course in Miracles* questions the conclusions, assumptions, and opinions in which you are caught. What would free you from your concepts and beliefs but the Action of Love? If you are already perfect, then all you need to know is who you are.

The action of the *Course* is the Action of Love. The *Course* awakens you and brings you to your own Identity. Something is happening in you. You begin to see, "My God, this is fantastic. The *Course* is not teaching me. It's making me aware." It doesn't influence because it is an action of the awakening of Love. Love is independent and It must therefore offer independence.

When most people teach, they want you to conform to their belief system. Your agreement gives them comfort and attention. But their teaching cannot be without motive. The human thought system never functions without motive because it is always unfulfilled. Only in Love is there no unfulfillment. Love alone is independent because Love alone is of God.

A Course in Miracles has no vested interest. It relates you with your own Identity. You step out of the world because you are not of the world. You are outgrowing everything that is born of time. The human thought system is of time. But somehow just the touch of awareness that you are eternal takes away the pressure.

> *If it helps you, think of me holding your hand and leading you. And I assure you this will be no idle fantasy.* [12]

These are the words of Christ. And this promise is met in every single lesson. Each lesson is consecrated and blessed.

Your attitude begins to change. You gain strength and confidence and faith. The *Course* speaks to you and assures you that you can make it. The system can't make it, but you can. What a gift of God! You can make it!

The Introduction to *A Course in Miracles* says,

> *This is a course in miracles. It is a required course. Only the time you take it is voluntary.*

*Free will does not mean that you can estab-
lish the curriculum. It means only that you
can elect what you want to take at a given
time. The course does not aim at teaching the
meaning of love, for that is beyond what can
be taught. It does aim, however, at removing
the blocks to the awareness of love's
presence, which is your natural inheritance.
The opposite of love is fear, but what is all-
encompassing can have no opposite.*

*This course can therefore be summed up very
simply in this way:*

> *Nothing real can be threatened.*
> *Nothing unreal exists.*

Herein lies the peace of God. [13]

The *Course* imparts the Divine Laws we have to
understand to come to peace and stillness. The only
choice you and I have is *when* we want to learn them.
While this is the curriculum, the *Course* does not
promote dogma. It shares with us Eternal Laws that we
lost sight of as we limited ourselves to ideas.

A Course in Miracles encompasses all religions.
Nothing is outside of it, just as nothing is outside of you.
It is God's gift to His Son, and it tells you the truth.
It is not concepts. It is not theories. It is not ideas. It
ends the fragmentation inherent in thought, and the
separation between you and God. It says that God's
Will is your will. When you begin to discover that,
you fall in love with the words of truth. Just to hear

those words changes you. Just by hearing you are transformed. The *Course* introduces you to your own sacredness. Without sacredness, this world is in chaos.

So, read it with your heart. It's just a lesson a day. Read the lesson in the morning. Bring to your remembrance your own Reality. Remembrance doesn't mean that you just think of the lesson every hour. What it really means is that you are declaring your freedom from time, from external pressures, and from the world of illusion and unreality, because you dare to remember that you are eternal.

Then you can say, *Peace to my mind.* [14] And time cannot touch it. Time cannot touch peace. No circumstance can intrude upon *Let all my thoughts be still.* [15] Nothing can invade the stillness inherent in you.

Make contact each morning with the lesson of the *Course* to revive remembrance of your sacredness. Then before going to bed, sit quietly, come to stillness, and read the *Text.* Within one year you will find your function. For you will no longer be threatened by what is unreal. Having discovered your Reality, that is what you will extend. And you won't make causes. Your likes and dislikes are finished. You won't have to belong to anything. You become the light. You become part of that which is Universal. A liberated being brings salvation to all humanity. And you, too, have that potential.

So, wherever you are, whatever you are doing, start to make a little space. As you awaken your own potentials, the external circumstances will change by themselves. Your own wisdom will know what is right.

And anytime you are pressured, you can say, *Peace to my mind. Let all my thoughts be still.* Once they are still, there are no problems. The energy of stillness burns what is unreal, like a light that dispels the darkness. A still mind is the Mind of God. It is at peace, absolutely free of opposites. And a person at peace in a troubled world is very much needed.

Any problems? How can there be problems in Life? Any questions? It's the same thing.

Peace and stillness know no problems, have no questions, and accept no answers. For they are free of ideas.

CHAPTER TWO

Approaching Truth –
How to Read *A Course in Miracles*

How would you prepare, my friends, to communicate with the Thought of God? With what reverence? With what humility? In humility, you put aside your own thoughts, your "me and mine." You come to receive. Then you are close to the state of meditation, just because you are approaching the Thought of God.

Your peace surrounds me, Father. Where I go, Your peace goes there with me. It sheds its light on everyone I meet. I bring it to the desolate and lonely and afraid. I give Your peace to those who suffer pain, or grieve for loss, or think they are bereft of hope and happiness. Send them to me, my Father. Let me bring Your peace with me. For I would save Your Son, as is Your Will, that I may come to recognize my Self.

And so we go in peace. To all the world we give the message that we have received. And thus we come to hear the Voice for God, Who speaks to us as we relate His Word; Whose

*Love we recognize because we share the Word
that He has given unto us.* [1]

Let's talk about how to read *A Course in Miracles*.
Lesson 298 of the *Course* says,

I love You, Father, and I love Your Son. [2]

We think we know what this means. But do we?
Honesty is required to know the truth. As long as we
are content with just words – and most of us are – we
will never know whether we really love.

We use the word "love" so frequently, but few of
us have any notion of what it really is. Every single
word – including the word "love" – is external to the
actual state of love. Love is a state uncontaminated by
words.

Love renews itself all the time. How many billion
breaths are taken every second! Can you sense the
energy behind them? Every split second the planets are
rotating. With what energy! Can you conceive of it?
That is what love is: that kind of energy. The impact of
this realization dissolves all words. It brings one to
innocence, to the purity of a saint. And probably the
saint alone has the right to use the word "love," and no
one else.

As long as we keep using words without knowing
the reality behind them, we are never going to know the
power of *A Course in Miracles*.

Our reading is no reading at all.

*   *   *

Over the centuries we have learned to want more and more. And now this mania for wanting regulates our lives. Whether it's property, friends, or knowledge, we want more. That is the function of the brain – to project a want and pursue it. We are victims of "moreness."

The first thing the man of God discovers is that the brain is always pursuing activity. The realization of this fact brings him to stillness. He has touched upon a truth. That moment is eternal. And whatever he utters at that moment of stillness is part of eternity.

The man of God comes to a still mind because he has seen through the deceptions of thought. What do you think he discovers? This may shock you. He discovers that we can't learn. Our "learning" is just the mania for self-improvement. We are already perfect, but we think we are not. And therefore, all our learning is an indulgence. But we don't want to give it up.

Truth is something totally different. Truth is uttered by a state of being. As we free ourselves from illusions, we discover that ideas have no meaning. They have no validity. Any person who is regulated by ideas – and most of us are – is unstable and unfulfilled.

We cannot read *A Course in Miracles* as long as we are caught in ideas, because the *Course* is not an idea. It is not abstract. Its words are uttered from the actuality of the state of love. And the purpose of these words is to bring us to it.

* * *

We value education and affluence, but look at the consequences. Never have we been so exhausted. We consume our nervous energy in wanting, stimulation, and conflict. And the planet itself is worn out.

Even seeds are losing their vitality. And seeds are not of time. A seed is eternal. You can save it for a thousand years and it doesn't age. But now, everything is depleted.

Can you step out of the momentum of tension and activity? Can you make some space in your life? Start simply at first. Put some time aside when you can relax. Give yourself a break and really rest.

It is going to be difficult to stop projecting and pursuing images. It takes integrity and courage, tremendous wisdom and strength. It's so easy to read the newspapers. It's so easy to say, "Let me telephone so and so." It's so easy to become a "do-gooder." Can you put all your projections aside, just for an hour? Get to know yourself, just for an hour? Then, after you have relaxed, recuperated, and stopped projecting, you will find something new within you.

And if you fall asleep, sleep. Be kind to yourself. Don't go for the "more-ness" of meditation; you won't find it anyway. First, be kind to yourself. Get somebody to give you a good massage.

Find some time to read the *Course* from a relatively still state. Slow down. Don't hurry to read the next sentence. You can know the reality – not just the words. Give yourself enough space not only to read the words, but to harness the energy of the truth behind them.

You will see how the *Course* intensifies your stillness and awakens divine faculties. This awakening is so sweet, so delicious, so energetic, you will no longer want to learn. Unless you awaken to this gladness within, you will keep searching outside of you. But your own gladness is independent of ideas, of anything external.

Then whatever you do expresses your goodness, the goodness given you by Divine Forces. You begin to realize you are not separate. You no longer judge others who are different from you because they have other ideas. You appreciate who they really are. You never conclude, because the minute you've concluded, you've judged. The minute you've judged, you've fallen into the trap of knowing. Retain your innocence. Innocence can listen and heed the still, small voice within. It can heed *A Course in Miracles*.

The *Course* is holy. It is sacred. Step by step, it brings you to the awareness of your own perfection, your own holiness. Then, whatever you do would be an extension of God. There won't be "you" in it. And it would be most joyous, affecting this planet for eternity. One moment of truth vibrates on this planet forever.

That is what *A Course in Miracles* is all about. Every single lesson brings one to that state, to the Mind of God. Every single lesson.

*   *   *

Obviously, there is a different way to approach and read the *Course*. We have to approach it with reverence. It is not just something you do.

How would you approach it? Pick up the book abruptly? Casually throw it here and there? Hurry through it? If you have a busy life style and want the *Course* to fit into it, you are not ready to fit into God's Mind. You have to see this deception.

You don't think you can change, but you want to improve yourself. And now you have *A Course in Miracles,* and you read it for its "good ideas." But the minute you reduce it to ideas, it is no different from anything else. Whether it's the Bible, the Koran, the Torah, or the Vedas, don't we reduce them all to ideas?

What is our approach to *A Course in Miracles?* Much depends on how we read it. (I have hardly met anyone who knows how to read.) We read words, but words are not the thing. Our words have meaning only at the level of unreality, the level where we project and pursue images. We find it difficult to dissolve our abstract thoughts. That would take a different kind of reading, a different kind of thinking, a different light.

Do you really want to step out of the mental preoccupation that gives you no rest? Do you really want to bring the brain to silence, to see its deceptions and illusions? Do you care enough for yourself to come to a different state? Can you give your full attention to reading *A Course in Miracles?* You have to challenge yourself. We rarely do that. And the "self" continues.

You have to see that you must die to the "self." If you have that burning need to awaken, your relationship with the *Course* changes. But if you are casual, you can read it over and over, and it won't transform your life. You can't be casual and say that the *Course* doesn't work.

Generally, we do things half way – half milk, half water. When we are not serious, our life becomes a ritual. And because the brain is lazy, it loves routine. Not only that, it thinks when it doesn't have to. It is not very intelligent. Our compromises create inner conflict.

To be free of casualness, we have to love what we're doing. What do you love or really care for? What is of first priority to you? Is it something for which you have reverence? Each lesson of the *Course* will confront you with such challenges.

But you and I don't have the time. We don't have the space. And probably, if you don't mind my saying so, we don't live rightly. Our energies are dissipated. Then when a challenge comes, we put it off. As Hemingway said, "Tomorrow, I can do everything." Tomorrow is our dumping ground.

To stop compromising requires urgency. Urgency brings you to attention. When the rattlesnake is right before you, you pay attention.

*   *   *

In the village where I was born in India, few children went to school; they preferred to play. In one family, however, the parents insisted their son get a good education. He attended the village school, the town school several miles away, high school, and college.

After several years, he returned home as a college graduate, well dressed and articulate. He had a different air about him. He was no longer a peasant, so to speak. He spoke English well and told us about his experiences. Everyone was impressed.

But soon the villagers discovered that he knew *about* things but he didn't know the thing itself. He didn't know the truth.

More shocking to the villagers, however, was that he was still greedy and selfish. They said to him, "You spent fourteen years in school and you're still selfish! What did you learn?" Can you see how the innocent are shocked? They thought education was meant to bring you to self-knowing, to purity and righteousness.

Now let me tell you a wonderful story from the *Mahabharata** that illustrates uncompromising integrity.

---

* The *Mahabharata* is the famous Hindu epic which tells the "… tale of heroic men and women, some of whom were divine. It is a whole literature in itself, containing a code of life, a philosophy of social and ethical relations, and speculative thought on human problems… He who knows it not, knows not the heights and depths of the soul…" From "Kulapati's Preface" to the *Mahabharata* by C. Rajagopalachari (Bharatiya Vidya Bhavan, Bombay, 1951), page 2. Editor

Once there was a king in India whose name was Yudhishthira. As a young boy in school, Yudhishthira was very clear and bright, totally present. He would come to awareness rather than to words. His teachers were very happy with him because he could instantly grasp a principle.

How does a wise person grasp a principle? He doesn't go through the labor of learning. He sees the principle instantly, gives it space, and allows the truth of it to unfold in him. And if he questions, "What is love? What is peace?" his question becomes a prayer. It has vitality. Because he doesn't compromise and accept his own words for an answer, awareness awakens in him. Will you do the same? It is your own words that deceive you. If you don't accept your words as the answer to your questions, you will come to stillness. And something else will flower in you.

So Yudhishthira did not learn through effort. One hint and he understood the principle. When he understood what love is, instantly he saw that everything is created by Love.

One day, the teacher introduced two lessons from the class reading primer. The book said, "You must never get angry. And you must never tell a lie."

The next day, his teacher began a new lesson. But Yudhishthira wouldn't read any further. This brilliant being was tongue-tied. His teacher said, "Maybe he has a tummy ache or something."

But day after day, it went on. Yudhishthira was stuck. His teacher was worried. His parents were worried. And even the other students were worried.

Finally, the teacher tried to shake him up. "Come on. Everybody else is reading. They're passing you by. What's the matter with you?" The teacher was so angry, he slapped him. "Come on! Over a month of this? You've only read the first lesson. Why won't you learn? What's happened to you?"

Yudhishthira said, "I have learned one thing: You slapped me and I am not angry. But I still tell lies." And he wouldn't go on until he had mastered that second lesson.

Are you going to read the *Course* that way? Will you be uncompromising?

A Course in Miracles can bring you to a state of being that is untouched by compromise. If there's urgency in your life, then we have something to do.

A very nice woman recently told me, "I have studied these books for six years and I still get angry. I can't become what I'm supposed to become through the books. Today I was crying. I understand the *Course,* but I can't really get it. I can see how the mind operates, or rather how the ego operates, but even though I can understand it, I can't let go."

This is everyone's dilemma, isn't it? Compromise gets the better of us. We need urgency to bring us to seriousness, to full attention. If you are serious, you'll see that compromise will never lead you anywhere, not in six years, sixty years, or six thousand years. If the brain can postpone anything, that's what it will do. The brain invented tomorrow.

We are all dealing with the same brain caught in its knowing that does not know. Carl Sandburg said, "There is only one man in the world, his name is All Men. There is only one woman in the world, her name is All Women. There is only one child in the world, his name is All Children."

To break free, we must come to a state that is uncompromising. But the difficulty is that we are too comfortable, we can afford to compromise. We are content with our answers. If we can't find the answers ourselves, then we find a guru or someone who is more clever, who gives us an answer that pacifies us. But that is not religious. Religion is a state of being. It is innocent and silent.

Real religion would make us miserable because our life is a series of compromises. We are afraid of crisis. We want to play it safe.

But don't condemn yourself. Just be the witness and observe how resistant you are to looking at yourself. How do you kill time? Where does your energy go? "Know thyself" is the beginning of wisdom. Put your idealism away. Get to know your motivations, your inconsistencies. And don't cover them up. Justifications are never valid. Find out whether you really want a religious life that is a state of being, and not a dogma.

You and I have to learn something called reverence. This is alien to the West, although the Orient doesn't have a monopoly on it. Without reverence, we will not come to silence. Reverence is a quality like gentleness.

You know when you love someone, how gentle you are? That gentleness brings about an atmosphere where you both open up to give and share something much deeper. You are thoughtful and your touch speaks. Caring civilizes you. It's something very beautiful.

Reverence for life includes respect for another and love for your own self. In reverence, you want to give. Without reverence, you want to take. In most sexual relationships, for example, we take from one another, using and abusing bodies to release tension. That is not reverence for life.

*   *   *

When I first touched the *Course,* it imparted something to me that is the most precious thing I have ever known. Something more precious than my own life, because without it, I didn't have a life. And therefore, I have reverence for the *Course* and never put it on the floor. When I travel, I don't lose sight of the carry-on bag in which I keep my *Course,* and I always carry it myself. I can't treat it as if it were just another book. Right relationship with it demands purity of me. For me, *A Course in Miracles* is the Thoughts of God.

When I read the *Course,* I hear God speak. It is not words then; it is something else. Something extraordinary leads me to the truth, the wisdom and the energy of the lesson. To see the truth of *My meaningless thoughts are showing me a meaningless world*[3] is to be free from all the world's commotion and plans. You are untouched by them. You can be in the world but not of the world.

To have a relationship with the daily lesson, sit quietly and give it space. Come to gratefulness and reverence so that you can receive the Thoughts of God.

Religion as a whole, throughout the ages, has put a lot of emphasis on concentration. But concentration means negation of everything else. It is isolating. Concentration requires effort and fosters self-centeredness. Can we see how organized religion promotes separation?

There is a difference between attention and concentration. When you are relaxed and attentive, you read the *Course* almost without pronouncing the words. The emphasis is not on words, but on what the words communicate.

Every word then becomes a law. And the depth of every line is a revelation. It takes one beyond understanding. It takes one beyond discovery. It even takes one beyond realization to the actual state of recognition that you are not separate anymore. Every single lesson dissolves the separation. Every single reading.

What a blessing to live for a year according to the curriculum of *A Course in Miracles*, the curriculum of God. But do it with reverence and give it space. When you are hurried, you can't fit it into your life. *You* have to change. And change is the most difficult thing.

That is why the real teacher has very few students. He insists upon their changing and they insist upon learning. And there is no relationship between the two.

A Course in Miracles is to be lived. Otherwise, it is like everything else we do – a preoccupation.

There are many scriptures and they are all holy. But none offers a step by step approach to application. Now we have this in the *Course*. Are you going to just read it without living it? Do you see the difficulties in bringing it to application? Mere understanding does not change us. The *Course* provides the vitality and benediction to bring it to application. That's what makes it the gift of God.

You can teach the *Course*, as many people are doing, but to really know the *Course* is a different matter. You have to go beyond your interpretation to discover the truth of it. You can think you're helping people and use the *Course* to earn a livelihood. But is that illusion ethical? The *Course* is not something one sets out to teach. To teach it one must first bring it to application.

*   *   *

Lesson 34 of *A Course in Miracles* says, *I could see peace instead of this*.[4] We all want to see peace, but what prevents us? It is hard for us to accept that we don't even know what peace is. We've known gratifying sensations and pleasure. But we have never known peace – an understanding beyond words, untouched by thought. It would have to be beyond words; otherwise, our thought would destroy it very quickly with fear or anxiety. Thought would take care of peace all right, even if we had momentarily touched upon it.

If you knew what peace was, you couldn't settle for anything less. It is so beautiful, so complete. Peace makes everything else secondary and trivial; you see it is an illusion and you can't be part of it. You can't be involved anymore. You trust the divine order of existence. And therefore, man-made fears and conditioning, likes and dislikes end – all duality ends.

What would be the action of peace? Obviously, its action would be independent of our personality. It would be an action of creation. There is only one Reality – the creative Action of Life. Plants extend it, birds in flight manifest it, planets in motion express it. They are all an extension of the same creative force.

By the time Lesson 34 comes in *A Course in Miracles*, we have seen *My meaningless thoughts are showing me a meaningless world.* [5] We have already gone through the challenge of *My thoughts do not mean anything;* [6] that disillusionment, that outgrowing has already taken place. And if it hasn't, then we have not given it the reverence, the attention, the space that is needed.

I could see peace instead of this means that we see Reality, and not what our thought is projecting. Haven't we always just seen what our thought projects? We think with thought and we look through thought.

When I read the lesson *I could see peace instead of this,* it means that I can let go of everything else. And if I can't let go, then I'd rather see my problem instead of peace. Some action, some decision, some transformation must take place. But we don't allow that. We stop short of peace; it remains a word. But the word is never the state, never the actuality.

Why don't we want peace? We settle for learning. I wonder if we ever learn anything. We need to end the illusion of learning in order to know peace. What a liberation to be free of it.

Peace is not of thought and it is not of personality. Personality wants peace and prepares for war. Militarism, national politics, and the drive for economic advantage are all inconsistent with it. Politicians play with the word "peace." No externals are going to give it to us – whether they be commercial, religious, or political.

Affluence is the poorest state of being. Anyone who is aware and objective sees our degeneration. Look at the pervasiveness of crime, drugs, and the disintegration of family life. We have no morality, no ethics, no eternal words in our lives that circumstances cannot affect. How few of us have our own water or even natural clothing. Things are out of control everywhere.

And when *A Course in Miracles* says we can have peace instead of this, we don't know what that means. We live a life of such stimulation. It's go, go, go – with no pause to step out of the momentum and hold hands with God. Where does our precious God-given energy go? While most families are struggling, corporations are rich.

Jefferson and other framers of the Constitution gave the New World a great gift in democracy. How far we've strayed from their vision. In Jefferson's time, you voted for someone you knew. You knew the moral principles by which he lived, you knew if his words were true. Today, you vote for candidates you don't really know. They must appeal to special interests to finance their campaigns. As a result, their inner conflict makes them incapable of peace. And you think they are going to lead the nation to it. Some kind of righteousness has to be there.

In the midst of this degeneration, the *Course* assures you that you could see peace instead of this torment and illusion, this world of unreality where you are helpless.

The Prince of Peace offers His Hand:

> *If it helps you, think of me holding your hand and leading you. And I assure you this will be no idle fantasy.* [7]

Have you a moment to hold hands with Him? When you do, you step out of time into eternity and you never return to time again.

By the time you've read the thirty-fourth lesson, you are responsible. You accept your function to bring all involvements and all loose ends to completion. You make right use of time; your life becomes productive. And you never solve problems with wrong means; you are thoughtful and loving. Your transformation relates you with everyone else because you exist in relationship.

Now you express your goodness and kindness. And you do nothing that is inconsistent. You see the ever-perfect Action of Creation helping you end your obligations.

You would be so pleased that, in everything, the Action of Grace helps you bring the false to an end. The "prodigal son" comes home. You look at the world's unreality differently. When you are at peace, that is how you see it – differently. You don't quarrel with it. You don't become a reformer, or make a cause, or interfere in other people's lives. You find another approach to life.

*   *   *

If you are going to read *A Course in Miracles*, everything has to change, beginning with your approach to the *Course* itself.

When you approach the lesson, you can read it as a duty, and then put it aside to get on with whatever you have to do. You can let the momentum of "me and mine" carry you along and read the *Course* when it's convenient. Are you honest with yourself when you do that? You couldn't possibly plan what you are going to do if you thought the lesson was going to change you. If you already have plans, you've decided that no miracle will take place.

Have you ever read the *Course* with no thought for what's next because you don't know what *it* is going to do? Is your interest in bringing the self and its plans to an end?

* * *

The great prophet Nanak, an extraordinary being, travelled all the way from Assam in India to Burma and to Mecca. Along the way, he freed people from their belief systems.

Nanak was always in trouble because he defied local customs. The Moslems, for example, were deeply offended when he slept with his feet facing Mecca. Wherever they are, Moslems make sure to sleep with their heads facing Mecca.

So Nanak does the opposite, and they correct him. "Turn around. Don't you know that your head must face Mecca?" They think he is feeble or blind. But he shows them who is blind. "Is there a place where God is not?" he asks. Simple question. "God is everywhere, not only in Mecca." They never bargained for that.

Nanak shows us that we, too, have to question everything.

Nanak's job is to free people from their knowing. He has outgrown words and man-made concepts. He represents the Unknown, the boundless Glory of God. He is a messenger of Love and Light, a man at peace.

Once Nanak encountered a priest who asked, "Would you meditate with me?" "So be it," Nanak replied. They sat down together. The priest said his prayers and then began to meditate. After some time, the priest got up and said, "Thank you." Nanak answered, "What do you mean, thank you? Did you meditate? All the time you were worrying about your colt falling into the pit. I thought we were going to meditate."

Nanak was right. While he was meditating, the priest was thinking about his new colt, "Oh God, I forgot to tie him up. He may fall into the pit. I should have told my son."

Do you long for each lesson to bring you a miracle that ends the past and introduces you to peace and timelessness, to the truth of your being? Then what is your approach to reading the lesson? Half-measures? Is it a duty, a ritual? We can read the whole book without ever having read the first lesson. And I wonder if everything we do isn't just the same: half-measures and half-truths. Are you totally present with anything you do?

Let us say there are two approaches to life. One approach continues the past and "me and mine." Your personality is preoccupied with its errands and its concern for survival. It pursues security and pleasure. It is driven by motives, always moving toward self-advantage. It promotes separation and buys all kinds of skills and religious and psychological phraseology to improve itself.

The other approach ends the past and brings you to newness. It invites you to end your rituals and half-truths. Let's call the approach of half-truths "activity," and the other approach "action." Action is of life; activity is of personality.

Action is something akin to prayer; prayer precedes thought. But we go to thought when we pray, and thought says, "Dear Lord,..." – whatever words we were trained to say. You may as well go for a bicycle ride. It's not a prayer; it's a ritual.

We settle for thinking, "I prayed." We're never going to see that it doesn't work. We would have to face "I didn't pray right," or "I'm a hypocrite," or "Why can't I pray?" We don't want to come to crisis. So we pray again tomorrow, without ever questioning if our approach is wrong.

Remember how Nanak said to the priest, "You didn't meditate. You were worried about the colt. Your brain was preoccupied." That priest would have gone on "meditating" without ever knowing what meditation is. Why do we lie to ourselves? To question our helplessness and hypocrisy – that would be a religious action, an action of Life.

*   *   *

There was a priest in India who took care of a little temple. His attitude was meek and his words good. Although a furnace of desire and ambition burned inside him, outwardly he was a professional.

By Hindu custom, before he would eat, the priest would prepare food and place it on a tray and offer it to the images of the gods in the temple. After blessing the food, he fed the gods and then he fed himself. He'd close his eyes in prayer, offer the food to the gods, bring the tray back and eat. Everything was okay. (Here, too, the system worked things in its favor. Everywhere in the world, if you open your eyes, you will find that business, politics, and religion all work to their own advantage.)

One day, something happened to the priest's son who was some distance away. The priest was in crisis. He had to go, but he couldn't miss feeding the gods. He didn't know what to do.

So he looked around and saw a peasant boy named Dhana in the field. Dhana had never seen a book; he couldn't read or write. "Dhana, come over here. I've got to go because my son needs me. Take a bath and wash yourself, and then prepare some food and feed the gods. I have to go, so this time you will have to do it."

Well, Dhana is scared stiff. He feels so crude, so out of place. He had never felt worthy even to enter the temple.

The priest was in such a hurry, he didn't explain too much. He just said, "Here's the tray, the food is in the basket. Don't tell me you can't do it. I've got to go." And he leaves.

So Dhana takes a bath. Then he cooks some food. And all the time he is feeling so inadequate he's shivering. Anyhow, he prepares the meal and takes it to the gods in the temple, rings the bell, closes his eyes to pray, and chants, *"Ram, Ram."* But when he opens his eyes, the food is still there.

He says to the gods, "I know I'm good for nothing, but please have mercy. Eat the food. The priest will be back tomorrow. Just take this now." (You know, it's so nice to be innocent.)

The food is still there. Again he pleads. And he prays a little more slowly this time. But the food is still there. He says, "Oh, I'm so clumsy."

So he goes and prepares another meal, now with even more care. He puts everything he knows into it, praying all the time. Men don't cook in India, but here he's got the job. He says to himself, "It's late, the gods must be hungry." He offers the food, sits down, and really prays. But when he opens his eyes, the food is still there.

And he says to the gods, "Please. I know it's not so tasty, but it's late, and you must be hungry." But nothing happens.

He wishes he were more sensitive. He wishes he could cook. He wishes he could do all kinds of things.

Then he bows his forehead to the floor and he really prays as hard as he can. "The priest will come back. He told me he would. Just eat one meal." But when he looks, the food is still there.

Now he doesn't know what to do. He has no other plans but to get that food eaten by the gods. So he goes and gets the kitchen knife. And he says, "I can't go on living if I am so bad that you won't accept my food." For him, the future has ended. Now they have a priest for a change! And he takes the knife and he says, "Either you're going to eat that food, or I'm going to kill myself."

And the food disappears.

Instantly Dhana became a saint. His tomorrows had finished. He had come to wholeheartedness. He put his whole being into his task and discovered that wholeheartedness is religious.

If you don't approach your computer brain for answers to your questions, words may be given that are not of thought. Never be deceived by your own knowing. Be willing to receive that which is given you to give.

When you receive what is given to give, you are unlimited. Your resources are boundless. You no longer calculate. All the resources of Heaven and the universe are yours to give because you have learned to receive.

Then you discover what Jesus meant by "Love ye one another." In reality, the only thing God shares is Love. You discover love is the only thing you and I can share. Nothing can touch it, nothing can frighten it. Nothing can buy it. When you have love to give, you are of Heaven. You are rich. You don't need education. If you have it, all right. But nothing else is necessary.

Dhana had no education. He literally believed that the gods needed to eat. It's so beautiful to be innocent. We are too clever. Which of us today could be Dhana? The priest said, "Feed the gods." Dhana came to wholeness, and the gods had to eat what he offered.

So, there is an approach of wholeheartedness. Most of us have known only partial actions in our lives. Now that we have the Thoughts of God offered by *A Course in Miracles,* could we please be wholehearted? Your offer of wholeheartedness can receive the miracles in the lesson, the truth of the lesson. To wholeheartedness is given the glory of that lesson and its peace.

Peace liberates man from his own bondage. We need to be liberated from ourselves. But we can never escape through political or economic systems, or organized religion. Our only function upon this earth is to discover our timeless Identity – that we are extensions of God. And we are not to hold another's "wrong" against him. We are to love one another.

We are offered the Thoughts of God to outgrow our man-made thought system of right and wrong. This system is based on self-centeredness and separation: I must look after myself; I must improve myself. The Thoughts of God say: We are all an extension of One Life, and we can see peace instead of separation.

Wholeheartedness brings us back to the awareness of our own Identity. How grateful we would be to know that It has always been there, but we have been absent. Our Identity is an extension of rightness unaffected by anything external. Neither atom bombs, nor earthquakes, nor economic depression, nor unemployment can touch a person who is with rightness. With rightness comes integrity and conviction.

A Course in Miracles is given to man at a time when he has become dependent on militarism, commercialism, and politics, all of which have gone berserk. Could we turn from the external to the internal action of God? There is hardly any hope for society, but there is hope for the individual to find peace within.

> *I could see peace instead of this.*

Peace is inherent in us, yet we manufacture anxiety. We resort to hate and fear and war. These are not of God. Love is of God. Can we afford it?

We have to take that responsibility – each one of us. Wherever you are, it's possible. Whoever you are, it's possible. Once you come to peace, whoever you thought you were is no longer real to you. Comparisons end and your preoccupation with "me and mine" is over. When you are at peace, that is what you give your neighbors, your children, your wife, your husband. This is the peace within you – not the peace one talks about.

You affect the entire atmosphere of the planet with your peace. When you have it, the trees know it, and the land you walk upon knows it. One person changes everything in creation. One Jesus who says, "I have overcome the world" [8] offers His hand to each and every one of us to do the same.

At peace, you are endangered by nothing external. And in this feverish world of panic, fear, and pressure, you can hold someone else's hand, too. You have space to listen to their problems. All problems are born out of a helplessness which is not real. You can tell the other person, "I am with you. We can cope with anything." Where two or more of you gather in His Name, Heaven is with you.

We have not yet known the power and the glory of peace. We could never turn to armament or to cheating or to falseness, if we were at peace. It brings simplicity into one's life. It uproots all that is unessential. It offers space and freedom from time.

Every single lesson of the *Course* offers peace. You don't have to be dependent on anyone. Your daily lesson is your daily bread of Truth.

Each day, as you eagerly go to the lesson, its gladness unfolds in you. And wherever you sit becomes holy. You make the room neat. You begin to see, "My goodness, I don't need this." You want to get rid of things, but you don't just throw them out. You find someone who needs them. Everything you do is an action of care and love; it is born out of rightness because you are not pressured anymore.

So, simplicity comes into your life and, with it, the Light of Heaven. As you sit quietly at peace, the very room changes. Everything is blessed by the peace of God, by your peace.

A *Course in Miracles* is not words. It is a state of being that is beyond words. Inherent in the *Course* is the blessing to bring us to that state. It is the greatest gift. Approach it with love and reverence. Give it your whole heart.

CHAPTER THREE

3

The Challenge of Living
A Course in Miracles

There is a very lovely prayer in *A Course in Miracles* that begins:

Into Christ's Presence will we enter now...

Here, "Christ" refers to a state of being, not to the man Jesus. The Christ state is within you and accessible to you, if you want to find it. Jesus was one person who demonstrated the Christ state.

Into Christ's Presence will we enter now, serenely unaware of everything except His shining face and perfect Love. The vision of His face will stay with you, but there will be an instant which transcends all vision, even this, the holiest. This you will never teach, for you attained it not through learning. [1]

See how beautiful this is:

You attained it not through learning.

*   *   *

A Course in Miracles cannot be taught; it can only be shared. What is the difference between teaching and sharing? When people teach, they lecture on a subject they've learned. Generally, they offer information *about* something, about the Roman Empire or about the fish that live at the bottom of the sea, things like that. Information is about all we have. And if someone else has spent more years than we have in the accumulative process of listening to lectures or reading books, we think that person is ahead of us or better than we are.

Information can be interesting, but if you didn't have it, it wouldn't make any real difference in your life. Greed is still greed, and anger is still anger, and fear is fear. These remain within us whether we are educated or not. We have listened to endless lectures at home, in school, at work, in the media. But we continue to indulge in the mundane and degenerate through drugs, violence, and other outlets.

Sharing, on the other hand, is different. It is not an accumulative process. It is not a one-way thing. Sharing demands your attention. What do you think attention is, in reality?

When we are not fully attentive, we settle for everything other than wholeness – for this or that person, place, or activity – and only the process of accumulation is at work.

But when we share, we come to attention. Attention is not intruded upon by thought; therefore, it flowers into awareness and awareness is impersonal. For the first time you let go of fear and the accumulative process. You outgrow all lectures and other people's ideas. You find what you were looking for within yourself.

Awareness is the only thing one can share. And where there is awareness, there is a Divine Presence. In real sharing, you and I share something eternal. When we come upon something eternal, we are silenced. It can be embarrassing because we dislike challenges, we dislike having anything demanded of us.

But if we do not call upon and touch the Unknown, then what are we going to share? Exchanging views and opinions is not sharing. We limit ourselves when we cannot go beyond our own, or someone else's, opinion.

We are all experts at avoiding challenge. Fashions change – hair, clothes, music – but we don't. We resist any challenge to the accumulative process of learning and wanting more.

Regardless of the society in which we grow up, we automatically accumulate its prejudices and opinions. The Italian remains an Italian, the American an American, and so on.

And then comes industrialization which says your beliefs are your own affair. But to make a living, you'd better learn the technology of business. So the Hindu, the Moslem, the American, and the Japanese adopt a commercial culture. And the driving force behind it all is still just accumulation.

Why is accumulation so enticing? We want to improve ourselves. It's questionable whether we ever really improve. Yet we like to accumulate; and therefore, we value the ideas and opinions of other people.

*   *   *

When one person in a million shares rather than lectures, he shares his awareness. There is a Divine Presence. On the other hand, we assume the one who lectures knows more and we know less. We like that. It makes no demand on us. When we meet scholars and religious people, we think they know. But they are mere interpreters, talking about something they learned from another. Generally, it is not their direct discovery.

✔ Awareness is not interested in information *about* things. Awareness is not only of this physical world; it is of the Source behind the world. Awareness brings something of another dimension to the three-dimensional human being. Only when we come to stillness can we know awareness.

If we don't make space in our lives, we can't come to awareness, and therefore we deny ourselves wholeness. Awareness is not limited to time or space. Awareness is of One Life, One God.

What you can accumulate is never real because when you accumulate you are not free. Freedom is in awareness; and awareness is not interested in accumulating. In that freedom of awareness, you learn the daily lesson of the *Course*, the reality of it. The lesson imparts its blessing if you are attentive.

Make space in your life – some space where there is no intrusion, where you are peaceful and still. Then read the lesson so you can communicate with what is eternal. The only thing you can do is give it attention. Once you give it attention, the brain is still. And you have received the gift.

* * *

The function of a real teacher is to challenge. There is nothing to teach, don't you see? As long as we are insecure and fearful, we can't learn, we just accumulate words. Without fear and insecurity, how differently we would look at the world!

Those who are insecure are often very clever and intelligent in the ways of the world. It is difficult to bring them to innocence and gratefulness.

We find ourselves asking, "Why does the teacher confront me? What is this negativity of his? Doesn't he like me?" We want a teacher who tells us how nice we are and gives us a lollypop. And the next day hands us another one, a different color.

These are the things that the real teacher confronts. He confronts them because he knows who you are. You think you need a guide, a teacher, some method. He says, "No, no, no." The real teacher knows that you are perfect.

But the one who teaches and preaches doesn't know anything about perfection. He says, "Look, I'm going to give you a method." Don't we all go for that? Don't we always project an image and then pursue it?

Unless we see that this is what we do, we cannot put an end to it. That's a big challenge. We don't want to go near a teacher who demands this. And yet we all say we want to change.

As long as we value our projections and our "knowings," nothing the teacher says really gets across. Why don't we see how resistant we are. That would be a miracle, wouldn't it?

What I'm trying to communicate is that the real teacher has to challenge. Jesus did. Mr. J. Krishnamurti did. I'm sure Lord Buddha did. And *A Course in Miracles* does, too.

The teacher must challenge you because he knows that any means you want to use to arrive at truth or awareness is false. To project a state of consciousness and then want to be there cannot work. There are no means to it. It's not from here to there. There is no "there" because there is no tomorrow.

The preachers and the gurus sell you tomorrow, don't they? "Do this, this, and this, and then you'll get there." And the schools train you in these methods.

The real teacher discovers that humanity is lost in this activity. Can you appreciate this insight and thank the teacher for it? Maybe it took centuries to discover this one pearl.

In ancient times, wise people were very selective. They only shared truth with a person who could contain it, who would not abuse it, who would not commercialize it, or draw attention to himself. Then that student himself came to freedom; he realized the truth and was finished with striving. He was a light.

But we want so much to accumulate knowledge. Why? Partly because we think we're nothing. And indeed we are nothing as long as we are not related to the reality of who we are. Only God and His Will and His extension are real. Nothing else matters. All human beings then are one and the same, aren't they? Status doesn't matter.

If we are insecure, we think someone is great because he has written a few books. When we've outgrown status, we see it is just part of the meaningless world with its meaningless thoughts.

So, the real teacher is the one who challenges. He challenges us to introduce us to our own perfection rather than put an extra coat of paint on us.

We don't like that. We say, "Leave me alone! Don't take my projections away. I can't live without them. What are you doing to me? How am I going to make a living?" Fear is not going to let go of us.

The real teacher knows the perfection that God created in you – not as an idea, but as a truth. Anyone can say, "In truth we are all one." But we don't know what truth is. In truth, there are no two. Unless this is realized, it's just an idea, it's a lie. Get it? Ah! Don't buy anybody's lies, even though lies sell like hotcakes.

The teacher sees that you are perfect and he introduces you to that perfection. How could he do that except by challenging your belief system?

Then he says: "All right. Now you have to challenge yourself to discover your own perfection. You have the resources. You can do what I have done. And so, go your way. Now you can help others."

The real teacher doesn't make anybody dependent.

*   *   *

The teacher gives rebirth, the birth that parents can't give. And now *relationship* comes into being, where before we knew only *dependence*. The teacher works only with those few people who are ripe. That is why he never becomes a public figure. He has no ideas to sell.

In ancient times what reverence people had for that kind of teacher! Not the teachers who taught mathematics and geography. The real teachers were so different. And they did simple things like weaving.

In my early twenties, I spent four years in the Himalayas in meditation and spiritual practices. When the anniversary of the birth of a great prophet came, many traveled to his birthplace to pay homage. I went too, with a group of other serious young men. We didn't tell lies and we didn't look at girls. We did the rosary and read the scriptures; we were good people. Sometimes we laughed. Most of the time we were very prayerful.

Five or six of us lived a very simple life together. I don't remember ever carrying anything. Isn't that nice? Perhaps just a shawl. When it was cold, I put it on; when it was hot, I took it off. It was so simple. Everything was provided. It was a different culture.

On the morning of the prophet's anniversary, a real Christmas day, we got up very early to go to the temple. Prayers started at two or three in the morning. And your status in people's eyes was determined by how early you rose.

And so we got up good and early. We wanted everybody to know who we were. Listen, status isn't only acquiring money and having a big house. The ego can find status in all kinds of things. The poorest man can find status. My friends and I had nothing but our nice big status and our egos – all draped in spirituality.

There was a saint living in a little hut nearby. He just stayed there; he didn't own anything. We all knew of him. "Let's ask the saint if he wants to go to the temple with us," one of us suggested. "That's a good idea." At least then the saint will know we're serious. Up early.

It's always a little difficult to approach such people – they have a kind of aura about them, a certain dignity. We went round and round about who would go and speak to him.

Anyhow, we were together, and togetherness gave us a kind of strength. The young are never courageous; they are daring. There's a vast difference between being daring and being courageous. We were daring. We didn't know what courage was. Not yet.

So we went and opened the door very gently. And we saw the saint sitting in meditation. It was really quiet. We said, "Santji, we are going to the temple to bow. Would you like to come?"

There was no answer. We waited. And we waited. And we waited. And then he said, "I went to the temple once and bowed my head, and I have never raised it since."

Another light, isn't it? He ends all the words, all the ritual. Some confronting! You could write a thousand-page book on it. The man says there are no means to it. The knowing and the searching have ended in him.

The real teachers have unique ways.

*   *   *

In studying *A Course in Miracles*, can we approach the lesson with the intention to end all thought? Each lesson has the vitality to free us from our seeking and knowing. It offers a joy we have never known before. Once we know that joy within, we will not go for pleasure or for gain. And we need never succumb to the daily routine. When we are empty, we seek fulfillment outside ourselves. It's a kind of curiosity.

So, now we come back to the real teacher – the teacher who challenges all deceptions, conclusions, and resistances. He is not going to be a favorite with those who are not really earnest.

Instead of being put off or resistant, why not discover the truth of what he is saying? The truth would impart its joy. Every challenge has enormous happiness to impart. It is not a threat, it is a joy. If you resist what the teacher says, it becomes a challenge. If you don't resist, it's a boon. A challenge is only a challenge where there is resistance. Isn't that beautiful? Now you have your own barometer: Am I resistant or am I joyous?

It is a joyous undertaking to question your assumptions and free yourself from your conclusions. We have deprived ourselves of that happiness, of that light. It is the only thing that is religious.

Jesus said, "Love ye one another." [2] In twenty centuries how many people have heard this and brought it to application? Nobody, whether he is religious or not, is against something as flowery as "love." But who has ever honored "love ye one another?" What about our motives? Our motives won't let us love another. What about our choices and preferences? They won't either. But what if we really knew love?

Do you know the difference between God's Thought and human thought? God's Thought challenges human thought and dissolves it. Then what remains is God's Thought. God's Thought is the only teacher.

Did you know that God's first Thought continues to manifest in creation? That same Thought still vibrates in us as His co-creators. We are the Thought of God and, as His children, we can know this. But we have never heard our vital, real thought. We don't want to hear it.

Without knowing our real thought, we will never know truth, love, creativity, or security. Our false knowledge is the block. And we are afraid to let it go. But the teacher says, "Challenging it is joyous; joy comes only when we are free."

*   *   *

I think the most essential thing in one's life is silence.

What is silence? We think that if we are quiet, we are silent. But we must come to silence without desire and wanting; otherwise, we are not silent.

You say to yourself, "I'm going to meditate and be silent." And then if you don't get high, you're disappointed. But if you do get high, you don't know whether or not it's your own projection.

You may not come to silence, but you'll enjoy telling everybody about the "light" or your "inner teacher." Just leave those projections alone.

Move toward discrimination and the simplicity of not wanting anything. Step out of stimulation. That would be the right thing to do.

Get to know yourself. See what is meaningless in your life. Notice what you do because you are unhappy and lonely and bored. Discover how loneliness and boredom rule you. You will find that without the unessentials, you think you will die. Ninety percent of our shops are sustained by the loneliness of people who already have too many clothes, too many shoes, too much everything.

If you burn within, you will weed out the unessentials. Then you will have space you won't know what to do with.

I will not value what is valueless. [3]

Loneliness has a sister called fear. They hold hands and dance. The two together totally control us and they rule the external, man-made world. As long as we're preoccupied with them, we will not be related to the God-created world. To recognize the God-created world requires wisdom, simplicity, and discrimination. What changes is man-made. What does not change is of God. It is eternal.

You can learn through your own wisdom. And then you will discover what you really need is in God's Hands. And you leave it there.

* * *

Not long ago, a child wasn't pressured to go to school so early. He developed a kind of harmony. He still had something of his own – his own inner music, his own discoveries, his own stillness. And, therefore, he wasn't overly conditioned by the externals. Now his stillness is shattered. "Go to school." "Watch TV." And it's getting worse and worse. We are being crippled.

It is essential that we make some space within. Sit quietly in silence and observe what takes place. How long does it take you to come to silence? The brain goes on and on, but stay with it; don't be impatient. Don't say, "My brain won't leave me alone," and activate it all the more. Just leave it alone. The function of the brain is to bring all illusions, all confusions, and all contradictions to attention.

Before you go to bed, take time to notice all the unfinished business of the day so it can be dissolved. When you sit quietly, you will find things you need to do that you forgot because you didn't give yourself the space. "I need to call the dentist. I didn't get to the bank. Ah, I could give my niece that silver tea set."

Don't be agitated by this. Let the brain do its reporting. A day will come when the brain will report in the first five minutes all you need to do, and you'll be grateful. Your brain will come to stillness because it has nothing more to report.

Then you will learn never to take on anything that you're not going to see through. You won't write a letter that's unessential. You won't use words that are sentimental lies. You will become a responsible person.

When we are busy, only one part of our brain is active. When we sit still, we awaken other parts of the brain and bring it closer to wholeness. Did you know that all thoughts have gaps between them? When you're angry, they get shorter. When you hate somebody, there are hardly any gaps at all. Sitting quiet would widen the gaps between our thoughts. This is a natural process. As the gaps widen, another energy comes into being. That's the sign of relaxation.

This other energy brings about a mutation in the brain. It may not happen the first day, or it could happen right away. But stay with sitting quiet; it will help you master your habits, impulses, and urges.

As these gaps widen, your brain cells are energized by silence. This is the same energy that otherwise is burned in thought, exactly the same energy.

You will feel at peace as the gaps between the thoughts widen. And these wider gaps bring you to the present where you become a witness to what is happening. But you never get involved.

The gaps are timeless. They come when you're relaxed, when your thoughts are less active. Through these gaps come certain clear moments that are far swifter than thought. You could have been thinking about something for two days or two years and, in one split second, it becomes clear. The gaps offer wisdom.

These gaps eventually begin to silence thought. First, they widen and give you energy. Then they begin to dissolve your thought. You say, "My God, how could I have been such a fool? They seem so superficial, these meaningless thoughts." They begin to drop away.

You come to a different energy within you. It's the light of eternity, the light of creation. Physical eyes don't see this light. Our physical eyes see only the gross, the dense – rocks and trees, you and me. Our "knowing" is limited to physical sight and to abstract ideas which judge what we see: I like it, I don't like it; this is good, this is bad. But this other light sees that which is of God. It is holy. It is a light untouched by time, not limited to space. It undoes the bondage in which you are caught. A few moments of this light are worth all of one's life. You feel as if you have lived, that you have seen the glory.

You are then the Son of God, extending the Light of Heaven. The Son of God does not live by man-made rules or opinion. Free of fear and boredom, he is never concerned with survival; it doesn't even enter his mind. All is perfect. All is holy.

As the Son of God, you would never become a guru or anything like that; the issue of status doesn't arise. You never look down on another human being because you see him as God created him, radiant in his holiness. You realize that he can't see his holiness; the gaps between his thoughts are too narrow. He is highly stimulated; he does things he should not do and justifies doing them. You begin to see how caught he is in his own self-projected littleness.

* * *

We are here to extend Heaven and, for this, we need a body. But now we are so immersed in the body, so trapped in it, that we think nothing else is real. We are unaware that there is the Mind, which is independent of thought, independent of the brain.

The brain's function is to look after our physical body. The brain sees only separation; I am dedicated to my preservation and you are dedicated to yours. My brain can't feel your pain; if you're hungry, I can't feel the pang of your hunger; if you're thirsty, I can't feel your thirst. Each body has its own limitation.

The thoughts our brain projects and learns from one another keep us insecure and preoccupied with survival – worried about tomorrow. These thoughts are just ideas and they've taken us over.

We are not just the body.

In silence, we touch upon another clarity, the clarity of the Mind of God. We discover we are part of the Mind and the Will of God in which there is no separation. Nothing is outside of it. Only in this state can we know what Love is. Love is eternal. It is not of thought. It is a reality. Peace is eternal. It is a fact and a truth. Love and peace are not of time.

One such person in stillness changes the vibration of the whole planet. He has a blessing to impart. You can feel the presence of such a being miles away. He gives expression to the Word of God, but he need say nothing, he need do nothing. He has no projects. Just his being is enough.

The Word of God is always love, always true. It has nothing to do with religious forms and behavior patterns, dogmas or theories. It has nothing to do with the brain, nothing to preach, nothing to sell. It just sees the other as holy. It sees no other reality than *I am sustained by the Love of God.*[4]

Stillness is content every moment. It has no wanting in it. It is ever renewed by the Love of God, by the Light of Creation, the Source of Life.

*　　*　　*

Make space in your life so there is space between your thoughts. Then you invite the touch of His Grace.

Perhaps you could set aside a little place in your home where you can go and sit quietly – some small corner that's beautiful and simple. There is no need to buy too many things. Put a few flowers there, if you like. This is where you hold hands with God.

You can find pictures of people in an exalted state of being. These pictures or photographs should represent a state beyond personality. They could be of Jesus or Buddha, of anyone or anything. Beauty itself can bring your mind to stillness.

Gladness will begin to flower within you. Think of God. Talk of God. Make His Name real. The memory of His Name is already within you, protected throughout the ages. Your sitting quiet brings it more and more to your attention. And then you find that He's not outside, and He's not a Name. He just Is.

What is nonchanging and ever sacred is within you. Don't think you are a wicked sinner or a lowly worm; that just reinforces your opinion of yourself. God can't change His Mind. Love has no opposite.

In ancient times, the Greeks and Chinese, the Hebrews and the Hindus knew that virtue brings happiness. So that's what they taught: a virtuous life offers happiness. Today, we don't know the difference between happiness and pleasure. Pleasure is for sale.

We have this tremendous craving for pleasure, pleasure, stimulation, and pleasure. So much wrong has been done by our culture of affluence and accumulation. Virtue and ethics are gone.

We're not even wise enough to know that virtue leads to happiness. Once you're happy, your discrimination protects you from the false. Happiness is something you find only within yourself. It's not offered in anything you can buy.

The world needs your peace. When you have it, it surrounds you. Isn't that nice? You don't have to learn anything or go anywhere.

Start with yourself. Value virtue. Make your life one of service to others. Talk with the parents of young children in your neighborhood and find out how you can be helpful to the whole family. Tell them you are available if they need a baby sitter or other help. You could go to their home or the children could come to yours.

On the other hand, if you're a parent, you might look for older people in the neighborhood who are bored and lonely. Mother Teresa said that, in America, there are people so lonely they wish they could die. Why can't they baby-sit? The child would bring them joy. He is not only your child, he is everyone's child. Let's give him lots of affection.

If you meet a need directly and do not commercialize your giving, there is healing in your hands. When you really feel for another, that is your prayer. Just your caring – even for a moment – awakens the powers of healing within you.

God is not deaf. Reciting a lot of words is not a prayer. Love is the real prayer. It is effective instantly. When two of you become one, healing takes place.

*   *   *

Before you do anything, make sure it is consistent with His Will. The last prayer in the *Workbook for Students* shows you how.

> *This holy instant would I give to You.*
> *Be You in charge. For I would follow You,*
> *Certain that Your direction gives me peace.* [5]

His Will would give you the strength and the integrity to do only what is consistent.

You must be determined not to compromise. When you compromise, you affirm helplessness. Never believe that you're helpless. You are not. You don't have to protest to anyone, "I can't do that. It is not of God." Just stay with your own conviction. That's the voice of strength. You are somebody; you represent Heaven.

God is with you. When you love, when you are virtuous, you are not regulated by anything external. Live for something real and you will never feel badly about yourself. *Nothing real can be threatened. Nothing unreal exists.* [6] These words will become your prayer. Silence will free you from what is unreal. You will see that the light has been within you all the time. It's so beautiful to know you are *sustained by the Love of God.* [7]

*   *   *

In the morning, give yourself space. Start the day slowly, in a gentle, loving way. Wake up early because the body has energy then.

Give thanks for a new beginning. Prepare yourself to approach *A Course in Miracles.* Wash yourself. Be alert. You are going to receive the Thoughts of God.

Sit quiet. Find a position in which you can sit comfortably for a long time without moving around. Make the body still so that your mind can become still. Sit with a straight spine – that's the only condition. You may want to lean back at first, but you will see that once your spine is straight, you won't get tired. This posture is important. When the spine is erect, other energies flow through you and cure many diseases.

As you sit quiet, invoke the Presence. In the *Course*, it is intimated that Christ – Jesus Christ – is its author, the one who gave us this gift of the Thoughts of God. *A Course in Miracles* is a process of Atonement. Atonement means the ending of separation. In the *Course*, Jesus says, *I am in charge of the process of Atonement, which I undertook to begin.* [8] Jesus Christ ends the separation.

Then read the lesson of the *Course* with all the love in your heart. And if the *Course* asks a question, try to answer it. Don't ignore it. If you don't know the answer – which probably you won't – be still, and it will be given to you. This is a course in *miracles*. If you don't listen to your own words, the answer will be given.

As each lesson introduces a different vibration, it brings about your inner transformation without effort. You just have to be true to doing the lesson as prescribed. Then, every half-hour or every hour, as you repeat the lesson, it reminds you that God exists, and that you are eternal, not subject to the pressures of time. Can you welcome that? Just for a moment? It doesn't take long. This moment becomes your prayer.

Prayer is never the words that you utter, but your intent. Make the decision to discover that you are the child of God, and your yearning will bring you to that clarity and to that light. Don't let anything interrupt your reading of the lesson. If you are interrupted, don't blame yourself. It's all right. Start again.

Never hold a negative thought about yourself or others. Negative thoughts prevent clarity. They're like dark clouds within. You grope in the darkness you've created. Fear and darkness are not real. One moment of that light and they are all dispelled.

Be very loving to yourself. Rest well, eat well. Don't put yourself in the second place; insist upon right food. And don't get too busy with errands. They are unending. They'll go on, even when you're no longer here.

Discover how beautiful you are, how holy you are. Because you are giving yourself this gift, you are not dependent on anyone. Wherever you walk, you take a blessing with you. You bring the blessing of Heaven to earth. Be at peace; find time to be quiet; give yourself space and spread your wings, for you are not of the earth.

By discovering who you are, you will see the beauty, the holiness, and the eternity in others. In eternity, there is truly no *other*. There is only One Life in which everything is related to everything else. There is no fear, no insecurity, no tomorrow. It is a blissful, alive, energetic present.

Put away the fear of loss and gain. Have a garage sale and sell all the junk in your house. There is great wisdom in simplicity. Simplicity offers you space. Buy what is healthy and natural, and learn conservation. Put away wastefulness. We are far too wasteful.

Be simple. Fall in love with yourself and with silence. And in the evening, read from the *Text* of *A Course in Miracles*. Get closer to that which is real. Step into a state that is no longer pressured. And if you want to read something else, read books that are virtuous, not sensational. Read the Sermon on the Mount or other scriptures. Put your heart into it. The quality of your reading makes the difference.

Read Emerson and Thoreau, and don't go near newspapers. They just excite more and more conflict. Superior to all reading is your own quiet. Out of that quiet you can say, *To everyone I offer quietness.*

Pray for the world from your heart, *To everyone I offer peace of mind.* You must have peace of mind to offer it; otherwise, you are lying to yourself. What can you offer that you don't have? Learn the peace and goodness of gentleness so you can say, *To everyone I offer gentleness.* [9] Be different. Be yourself.

Pray for all people of all nations. Drop the idea that somebody is wrong and somebody is right. Where there is love, there is no enemy. Never see another as belonging to a clan, a race, or a political or economic group. There is no such thing. You have to outgrow this collective insanity. We are all human beings.

Pray for all government leaders – that they will make decisions consistent with love, consistent with life. Your prayers and goodwill have their effect.

Bless everything that lives and shares life with you upon this planet. Don't limit yourself; don't pray for a few friends and stop there. "Bless me and my wife, my son and his wife, us four and no more." That's not a prayer, that's prejudice. Pray for everyone.

And forgive people – especially those with whom you disagree. Nothing justifies disliking a human being who shares the same life with you. Sit quietly before you go to bed and send your love to that person. Close your day clear and at peace. The quality of your sleep will improve.

Get a good rest. Don't tire yourself projecting and pursuing illusions. If you are too busy, relax sometime during the day; twenty minutes is all it takes to feel completely refreshed. Be kind to yourself.

Fill your heart with gratefulness. A gladness will flower that you have never known before. Then you have something to give to the world: your gratefulness, your gladness, your joy. The world needs them.

You are blessed with the gifts of night and sleep, all the stars in the sky, and the awakening at dawn of an energetic newness within you. It's a very beautiful world, a world expressing God's perfection and the holiness of life. Why walk the sordid man-made world of opinions and reactions?

> *To everyone I offer quietness.*
> *To everyone I offer peace of mind.*
> *To everyone I offer gentleness.* [10]

If you are gentle, you offer gentleness. When you are at peace, that is what you extend. Take your peace everywhere you go.

PART II

CHAPTER FOUR

To the reader...

Now you are ready to accompany Tara Singh as he explores the first ten lessons of *A Course In Miracles*.

Sharing his own discoveries, Tara Singh shows you how to read the *Course* so that you can receive the miracles it promises. You will find that the first ten lessons challenge the very way you see and think.

For the complete content of each lesson, please consult the Course's *Workbook for Students* directly.

Editor

4

The Daily Lesson Offers Miracles

Will You Decide to Be Transformed?

A Course *in Miracles* exists to awaken you from the *sleep of forgetfulness.*[1] Its function is the ending of separation. When the *Course* says, *All the help you can accept will be provided,...*[2] it is referring to those who make an earnest commitment to themselves. Can you come to conviction and say, "I am a student of *A Course in Miracles?*" If you do, you will have a relationship with the spirit of the *Course* for life.

This is a decision you have to make. The decision is either to call upon the energy of the Mind or to remain with the energy of the body – the brain, the thought system of the ego. A decision is neither a choice, nor a preference. It knows no compromise.

Without decision, you will never discover the energy of the Mind – the Mind of God of which you are a part. You need the energy of the Mind to say, "I will not accept separation. I will undo the confusion, the sadness, the ingratitude of the brain. I will call upon miracles." This is transformation.

When you get into a mood or find yourself depressed and hopeless, the energy of the Mind will tell you that this is ingratitude. The Mind does not know lack. The brain will tell you that you cannot manage, that your situation should be this way or that way. It will always promote a lack and make you dependent on the externals. For inner correction, however, you can always call upon miracles.

> *We stand together, Christ and I,*
> *in peace and certainty of purpose.* [3]

Are you certain about your purpose? Without decision, can anyone be certain? Make your decision, and you will call upon the strength of the Mind. Your decision will affirm that you are not a victim of time with its illusions. When you, the Son of God, make that decision, you discover your own godliness, your own holiness.

This makes sense to us, yet we can't seem to come to determination. At best, we opt for enthusiasm which doesn't last. The pace of our development depends on our determination to stay with it. Being with it means entering into timelessness in which there is no anxiety, no fear, no separation.

It is neither difficult nor easy, but it demands freedom from attachment to the world of the senses. Letting go is the issue. There is nothing else to do but to let go. There is nothing to achieve.

A Course in Miracles has solved many of the problems we have lived with over the centuries. Even prophets struggled to glimpse the laws the *Course* shares: that there is nothing to achieve, that we are sinless. Has humanity ever received such a gift?

The *Course* makes it very clear that understanding is not necessary; it doesn't matter. We always thought it mattered. Our whole life has been dedicated to understanding. The *Course* says you don't have to understand the lesson, but you do have to practice it. In fact, you may even resist the lesson or find it annoying. That's all right. You can keep your opinion; your mind is not trained yet.

Try to live the whole day with the lesson. Can you discover for yourself that, whether you like it or not, your opinion is meaningless? Would that discovery not be of the energy of the Mind? If you hold to an opinion of the lesson, aren't you limited to the brain level and thus separated from the creative energy of the Mind?

If you are going to read the *Course,* you have to practice it. The practice itself will introduce miracles into your brain and bring about a new mind.

Practice and remembrance are synonymous. In fact, stepping out of your routine to remember the lesson is more important than what the lesson for the day may say. If you can't remember to do the lesson, does it have any meaning? Without your remembrance and practice, you are not being true to the *Course.*

The time given to complete the lessons is one year – 365 days. By the time you come to Lesson 50 and the review lessons which follow, the *Course* is moving you through an accelerated process. The Christ within becomes your Teacher. And in each lesson there are glimpses that you are part of the Mind of God. The separation never took place.

Now you begin to recognize that the *Course* is a spiral. At each level of the spiral, there is less of the brain and more of the Mind. As the "you" starts to decrease, the Christ in you starts to increase.

The first spiral helps you transcend understanding and master practice. From practice, you move to the second spiral where you become more and more aware of the Mind you share with God. This movement takes place involuntarily. All you have to do is be true to the practice.

So as earthliness decreases, holiness increases. What an action! Each spiral awakens different potentials that you never knew and never used. It introduces you to who you are as the Altar of God on earth, and awakens your capacity to receive the light of the Mind. The brain is transformed without resistance.

In the third spiral, you have fallen in love with the *Course* and will never let it go. Your attachment to things of the world begins to crumble. You no longer fit into the world of illusions as your remembrance of God, of True Knowledge, awakens.

Conviction and integrity emerge. And therefore, the brain's moods, depression, fear, and insecurity have little effect. Now you have goodness to give your neighbor, your wife, your husband, your sons and daughters. What is life without goodness?

Where goodness is shared, dependence disappears. You have the creative light of the Mind to give. And what you share is impersonal. First, you shared physical closeness; now you share goodness, gratefulness, love, and truth.

If you make practice of the lessons as prescribed your first priority, within one year you can be transformed. Will you be a student of *A Course in Miracles?* Will you make that decision?

Exploring LESSON 1

"Nothing I see in this room
[on this street, from this window, in this place]
means anything."*

      Can any of us say words which would be true ten years from now? A hundred years from now? What has happened to us? What good are all our inventions, our education, or the "isms" that determine our lives? We think what we see means something. But the first lesson of *A Course in Miracles* says: *Nothing I see... means anything.*

Because the *Course* requires a great deal of attention, after a time most people put it aside without ever making contact with the energy of its words. *A Course in Miracles* is True Knowledge. It would be significant if even five people applied it. After all, eleven fishermen changed the destiny of the world!

The very first lesson starts to undo our belief system.

Nothing I see... means anything.

---

* *A Course in Miracles, Workbook for Students*, page 3. [W-1. page 3.]

You would be liberated if you fully realized this. Why? Because if what you see did not mean anything to you, you would not be attached to it, it would not regulate your life. Does your bank account have meaning for you? Does it have power over you? Who gives it meaning?

The first lesson could free you from all you know. You make a mistake in believing that other people's abstract theories are your own thoughts. If you gave it space and attention, you would realize that what you know is not real, that you are subject to your conditioning.

You may try to understand the idea of the lesson intellectually but that does not mean a thing. Truth is independent of personality. Truth is not *about* something.

Why aren't we disillusioned with the insanity of our thought system? The very means by which we think is corrupt. And, within that corrupt framework, we want to have better thoughts. But *thoughts* cannot *be* better.

Nothing I see ... means anything.

What does nothing mean? If you find meaning in something, then it's not nothing. Ah! Is there a person who would not give meaning to anything? If you say, "Nothing means anything," then you must be able to come to that state. But you will say, "Look, I can't help it. I give meaning to everything I see. Everyone I know gives meaning to what they see."

Now look slowly around you, and practice applying this idea very specifically to whatever you see:

"This table does not mean anything."
"This chair does not mean anything."
"This hand does not mean anything."
"This foot does not mean anything."
"This pen does not mean anything."

Try to free your mind from giving meaning to what you see. Then I would say that you are applying the lesson. Just learning it is a substitute and very destructive in the long run.

Reading the lesson means having the capacity to receive a miracle. A miracle undoes the accumulated meaning the brain has given to what it sees. Learning is just accumulation, and in it there is never a miracle.

Nothing I see… means anything.

Nothing means "no thing." If you see "something," then you are fragmenting or isolating that "something" from the whole. But it is merely an image; it is not reality. And so the contradiction begins. One part of you says, "It's nothing." The other part says, "I see my hand. How can I say it's nothing?" You get into a mental controversy and miss the basic issue.

Observe your brain's activity. You will notice that if it comes to total attention, it does not interfere; when it is not interfering, you cannot give meaning to what you see.

You have to put energy behind attention. And then attention becomes the teacher that transforms your belief system.

Nothing I see ... means anything.

If you understood the meaning of the word "I," it would bring about a revolution within you. "I" encompasses everything when it is free from the limitation of "things." To that "I," everything is nothingness, and nothingness is liberation. Your "knowing" limits you; realizing the words of the *Course* sets you free.

The power of the first lesson is boundless. You cannot interpret it or you will deny yourself the Truth that corrects all errors in your mind. [4] You must insist upon making direct contact with the Thoughts of God inherent in the *Course*.

We know nothing other than appearances. And our hypocrisy doesn't bother us when we say, *Nothing I see ... means anything.*

Our own thought system has no validity. No idea or concept transmitted from one brain to another has Truth in it.

Thought itself is merely a substitute for seeing. When you distrust thought, you are moving toward clarity, toward awareness. But when you're moving through thought to clarity, you're deceiving yourself. We can see only the deception of our own thought. That is seeing clearly. Clarity, or awareness, is a different energy than the energy of thought. It undoes. It is creative.

Thought will never touch awareness. Awareness is not of the brain; it acts *on* the brain. Awareness is a moment – a miracle – that frees the brain from all it has learned and accumulated, from all the meaning it has given to what it sees.

Thought cannot know responsibility, or ethics, or the *Course*. We have to see the mischief and the motives in the thoughts we think. There is no love in them; they are self-centered.

But we can begin to decondition ourselves with the first lesson. If we don't do this, we will never know what the rest of the *Course* is saying.

Can you be responsible not to get taken over by thought? You begin to wake up just by becoming aware of thought itself. You are no longer as attached or reactive to what you think. *Nothing I see… means anything* introduces a miracle: there is a knowing inside you that is impeccable, free of duality.

In actuality, there is meaning only in that which is whole, that which has no name. Therefore, you cannot make an image of it; it is the Unknown.

You begin to discover the limitations of the known, and you see the Unknown at work freeing you from them. There is nothing to seek, but everything to undo. Something is cleansed each time you recognize *Nothing I see… means anything*. You are renewed.

Exploring LESSON 2

"I have given everything I see in this room
[on this street, from this window, in this place]
all the meaning that it has for me."*

The exercises with this idea are the same as those for the first one. Begin with the things that are near you, and apply the idea to whatever your glance rests on. Then increase the range outward.

Your eyes see a tree – but the tree is just your concept of something that grows and shelters life. You give it the name "tree." You see it is a beautiful tree, or that it bears fruit, and you learn all about it. That is part of the function of your brain.

But vision does not see the tree. Vision sees only wholeness. It cannot separate the tree from anything else. Only the brain gives names to different things.

We see through thought. Thought has desires and problems. Vision does not. The issue then is to be liberated from thought which we project. It is not part of creation. God did not create thought; God created vision.

---

* *A Course in Miracles, Workbook for Students,* page 4. [W-2. page 4.]

How can you liberate yourself from thought? To step out of the world of projected thought and undo what is meaningless, you need the Holy Spirit. Wanting the Holy Spirit to solve your problems, however, is the wrong premise. To the Holy Spirit, problems don't exist. If you want to make contact with the Holy Spirit, you have to undo your own problems.

Can you take a stand never to allow your projected thought to rule you? When you are really intent on seeing the meaninglessness of thought, the Holy Spirit is already liberating you and bringing you to vision. But if you are content with where you are, then you don't need the Holy Spirit.

You cannot approach the Holy Spirit wanting something because the Holy Spirit undoes whatever you want. You may have thought, "Now I'm going to have someone at my beck and call." No. The Holy Spirit is not a bellboy. He is not going to increase your misery; it is your wanting that trapped you to begin with. If you have really called upon the Holy Spirit, can you continue to live with your old values? The Holy Spirit dispels the illusions of wanting and seeing. When you value vision above all else, the Holy Spirit is there. Your own willingness to undo invites Him.

Can you see that to relate with the Holy Spirit a change of values must already have taken place within you? You are outgrowing the world by undoing it.

Unless we put our energy into it, however, we are not going to be receptive to undoing. We live at the level of duality – of like and dislike, "I want this" and "I don't want that." How much of the world we have to outgrow to discover that, in reality, there are no separate trees, separate religions, separate nationalities. As we move toward recognizing ourselves as God created us, the Holy Spirit is already there, already helping.

Remember Lesson 1: *Nothing I see... means anything.* We protest, "I have to justify my seeing. My seeing gives meaning to my existence. How am I going to live in the world? How can I deal with the issue of fear?" These questions are beyond like and dislike. The fundamental premise of everything we have made is fear and insecurity. The central issue is survival.

We justify seeing everything in terms of our survival. We give authority to the brain – to the body – and we ignore the spirit. This is the error the Holy Spirit corrects.

I have given everything I see...
all the meaning that it has for me.

Can you accept the truth of this? When you are freed from the limitation of seeing, you will outgrow physicality itself. Then, even though the body no longer controls you, the Christ in you still needs your body to bring the light of Heaven to earth.

Can you look beyond another person's body and recognize the Christ in him? Your physical eyes cannot do this; only vision can. Then you are seeing what God created, and the issue of forgiveness does not even arise. Do you really want, more than anything else, to go beyond the limitation of physical sight?

I have given everything I see...
all the meaning that it has for me.

Seeing with the physical eyes could be called judgment. We have an opinion about everything that we see, and every opinion is a form of judgment. "This is mine, that is hers. I'll wash my dishes, but I won't wash yours." The "I" is false. Because the false "I" gives meaning, what it sees is meaningless.

In the end we will realize that what we have given meaning to has no meaning at all. To see what is meaningless liberates you.

We have turned things upside down. We do not want to outgrow; we want to seek. But seeking is unnecessary. Outgrowing is the only thing that matters.

You cannot escape the undoing. And to undo, you need the Holy Spirit, who serves no other purpose. When you are willing to know yourself – and to know yourself is to know God – you need to undo and eliminate all your assumptions, all your opinions, all your knowings, all the things you don't like, and all the things you do. Everything.

The more attention you give to undoing, the more energy you will receive. You must refuse to conclude it is hopeless. The minute you conclude, you worship thought again. You give meaning to the meaningless, and you alone can stop it. If you are serious, you will not accept your own conclusions; you will not live under the authority of thought. You will never again say something meaningless and believe it to be meaningful.

Vision is part of reality. Its light is already inherent within you. Once you are liberated from thought, your reality is the light. In vision you become part of the whole – the whole universe. Conflict, contradiction, duality end. There is only "what is."

You have much to undo before you finish reading this second lesson. It can bring you to vision, right here, right now.

Exploring LESSON 3

"I do not understand anything I see in this room
[on this street, from this window, in this place]."*

Sit quietly a while. Invoke the Presence of
Jesus Christ, the Author of the *Course,* the One in
charge of the process of Atonement. Approach the
Course with reverence and stillness.

We live an externalized life in an externalized
world, where there is a great deal of stimulation. But
we can't all run off to do the lessons in a solitary place
in the forest. We have to do them wherever we are.

Because you are pressured and stimulated, you need
the *Course.* It is like taking a bath in the pure water of
a spring. You need to be cleansed of the pressures of
the brain to have the space for a miracle. Can you see
now why the early lessons insist that you slow down?
Whether you are doing it for the first time or for the
fifth time, giving the lesson space is the key.

Each one of us exists as a potential, although we are
not aware of it. We have the capacity to receive what is
of God.

---

* *A Course in Miracles, Workbook for Students,* page 5. [W-3. page 5.]

Religious teachers and "baby gurus" have tried to preoccupy us with "doings" – do this mantra, this practice, that prayer. The person who knows his potential, however, has outgrown everything external. Freed from his own personality, he has discovered the concept of "me and mine" is abstract; it is not real.

As we realize our potential to receive, we become attentive. The brain naturally comes to stillness and receives the miracle. The miracle dissolves all words and wantings, and brings us to fulfillment. Thus we outgrow selfhood.

Let's not fail to realize our potential by trying to improve ourselves. How can we improve upon what is perfect? Instead of realizing the perfection that we are, we start a counter movement of unfulfillment.

I do not understand anything I see...

Your potential to receive would see the world with a still mind. Your still mind would look at things without fragmenting them. It would not assign value to particular things or begin naming them. The minute you start naming them, you are giving them meaning.

Look around with that still mind, without naming anything.

Then when you listen to a friend's problems, you can come to that same stillness. You can hear what he is saying without any opinion or judgment. Otherwise, while he is speaking, your brain is agreeing or disagreeing.

You must bring that interpretation to stillness because you don't understand anything anyway.

Then maybe out of your peace you would say something that is wise, something born of silence and affection. Your space would give you wisdom.

I do not understand anything I see...

What a release to relinquish the burden of knowing!

The lesson begins:

Apply this idea...
without making distinctions of any kind.

Become aware of how the thought process divides everything. By giving a particular thing an attribute, or by learning its name, we think we understand it. But we don't. This tendency to make distinctions is what separates everything. And we call that separation "knowing." No wonder we don't understand anything.

Maybe the issue is in what we call seeing. You see *your* chair, *your* plant, *your* arm. Even before you see the chair, you see whether it's yours or mine. Is this seeing? Or is it attachment and judgment? It may have nothing to do with reality.

If you give one thing meaning, you separate it from the Whole. The Whole, the Source, is real. Your physical sight is not. You give significance to your attachment, but the Whole cannot be owned. IT IS. Your isolation into physical senses separates and blinds you. Are you regulated solely by the body's senses?

> *Whatever you see becomes a proper subject*
> *for applying the idea.*

> *I do not understand anything I see...*

Because the lesson is the truth, everything becomes a proper subject. Aren't you glad to be moving toward humility rather than toward the arrogance of "knowing?"

Pretending to "know" is the opposite of gratefulness. In gratefulness you would be inspired; you would not distinguish this or that as "yours." In reality, nothing belongs to you, not even your fingers.

And so the lesson frees you from identification with anything partial. You realize your vast potential, beyond time and space.

> *Be sure that you do not question*
> *the suitability of anything*
> *for application of the idea.*

The minute you question, you use thought. A real question, however, questions thought itself. Rather than activating your mind, your question silences it. Your still mind receives the grace of something beyond thought. When the mind is still, it does not judge.

> *These are not exercises in judgment.*

Thought is the lowest form of intelligence. <u>The minute you use thought, you judge.</u>

> *The point of the exercises is to help you clear your mind of all past associations, to see things exactly as they appear to you now, and to realize how little you really understand about them.*

What will clear your mind but awareness of what you are thinking? You must demand this of yourself to awaken your inner potential.

The lesson continues: *It is therefore essential…* The *Course* doesn't use words like "essential" lightly.

> *It is therefore essential that you keep a perfectly open mind, unhampered by judgment…*

Do you know how to keep a perfectly open mind, unhampered by judgment? There's a lot of homework, isn't there?

Some years ago, after doing the lesson, I wrote:

> Judgment is out of separation,
> thus the continuance of "what is" – separation.
> Emotion, too, is personal and physical.
> In separation, I do not understand anything.
> My judgment places value
> according to attachment.

> May I see insanity as insanity
> and, by so seeing, step out of it instantly
> without time-thought.

As the wisdom of this lesson begins to unfold, you will grow a century. You cannot be what you were yesterday.

Exploring LESSON 4

"These thoughts do not mean anything.
They are like the things I see in this room
[on this street, from this window, in this place]."*

I want to share something with you –
something very profound. But I wonder if it will be
received. If you don't have the "ears to hear," the only
thing you will hear is your own opinion. What I long to
share is beyond opinion, even beyond thought. It can
be communicated *through* thought, but it cannot be
received *by* thought.

What does it mean to receive? To receive is to
harness the energy of truth the very moment it is shared,
and instantly bring it into application for the rest of our
lives. But we believe in learning. Learning means
postponing. "I'm going to learn now and I'll apply it
later." That is how we create time.

These thoughts do not mean anything.

A shocking statement, isn't it? What is thought?
Ask yourself. We've used it all our lives. Is there
anything your thought could say that means anything?

---

* *A Course in Miracles, Workbook for Students*, page 6. [W-4. page 6.]

We need to see our irresponsibility, how we abuse words and make them meaningless.

Thought is reaction – favorable or unfavorable, positive or negative. It either likes or dislikes a person, place, or activity. It is caught in choices. Beyond assertion and defensiveness, what does thought know?

Before we become reactive or confused, why not be honest and realize that nothing our thought says means very much. It's just words, isn't it?

Now that this has been shared, have you received the truth of it?

Is it possible for us to discover directly that thought is *reaction* and that life is *action?* This discovery itself is an action, for action dissolves thought and sees the false as the false. Action can say, *These thoughts do not mean anything.*

Applying *A Course in Miracles* requires integrity and conviction. We have seldom demanded these of ourselves. It is very difficult for us to change. In fact, to change is the most difficult thing in life. If one person in a generation changes, that is a very fortunate generation. We don't seem to have the necessary passion for truth; we don't really *want* to change. We want to do things; we want to improve ourselves. Why do we lack the passion to apply what the *Course* imparts?

> *Begin with noting the thoughts that are crossing your mind for about a minute.*

How many thoughts occurred to you? Dozens, right? There is not one moment that you're free of them. But the one moment you observe them can reveal the pattern of your life because that moment is what your life *is*.

✔ What happens when you begin to note your thoughts? You discover that thought takes you away from yourself, it relates you with the externals, it is always *about* something. Awareness, on the other hand, brings you closer to yourself and shows you how you think. The action of awareness is much stronger than the action of thought, for awareness is a light that cannot be deceived. Awareness sees the false as the false.

Awareness does not "do" anything. It simply says, "Look, what you are doing is false." Can you recognize the false as the false, without doing anything about it? If you can, action is at work. To see the false as the false frees you from it. You are no longer part of it. However, merely to repeat these words and think you have learned them is not to be free.

If we deceive ourselves with "learning," eventually the potency of the *Course* is lost to us.

Thought promotes activity; the action of awareness undoes activity. Awareness discovers that only the Will of God is not false. To really see the falseness of personal life brings you to innocence. When innocence says, "I don't know," in actuality it is saying, "Thought does not know." Out of that freedom, a new expression is born.

The observation of your own thought awakens discrimination. Then "know thyself" comes into being.

> *You will find, if you train yourself to look at your thoughts, that they represent such a mixture that, in a sense, none of them could be called "good" or "bad." This is why they do not mean anything.*

You can now question the authority you give to thought. It regulates you; it has exploited and manipulated you all your life. Now you know what the problem is. And your observation of the problem makes you serious.

The lesson goes on to say these are not even our *real* thoughts.

> *Do not be afraid to use "good" thoughts, as well as "bad." None of them represent your real thoughts, which are being covered up by them.*

The thoughts that cross your mind are of personality. Personality's thoughts do not mean anything. Once you see this, they're out of the way.

You don't have to do anything about the real thoughts; they are already present. Real thoughts are those you think with God. They are of the spirit.

Learning, understanding, and knowing are of personality's thought. They do not mean anything. The clarity within you that dissolves thought is real.

You will come to know your real thoughts if you give yourself the gift of silence. You take a step to receive them by being attentive. When you are attentive, the thoughts that mean nothing begin to disappear. And automatically you become receptive to your real thoughts.

All you have to do is come to silence and observe the glory and holiness of its impersonal action. Silence introduces you to eternity which is always pure, always uncontaminated.

What a benediction to be born at the time of *A Course in Miracles,* to have in your hands the key to Heaven. Now, will you trust the words of the *Course* more than your own?

Exploring LESSON 5

"I am never upset for the reason I think."*

$\qquad$This lesson can liberate us from all depression, sorrow, and pain.

New energies come into being which make us more receptive to the blessing the *Course* brings to our lives. The awareness of this blessing helps us realize that we are never upset for the reason we think. Therefore, we need never be upset by anything external.

We all have a faculty or clarity called "reason" that can correct our misperceptions and reactions. According to Eternal Laws, the very function of right reason is to correct error. Right reason would show us that only our misinterpretations upset us.

Suppose you are jealous, angry, or fearful. At that moment, if you could say, *"I'm never upset for the reason I think,"* could you remain upset? Certainly not. These words would liberate you because they represent Absolute Thought.

_____
* *A Course in Miracles, Workbook for Students,* page 8. [W-5. page 8.]

You may accept this intellectually, but wait until you are involved in an upsetting situation. The last thing you are going to say is *"I am never upset for the reason I think."* You would rather have the upset than peace of mind.

We have to discover the cause of the upset and why we ascribe the upset to that cause.

> *I am never upset for the reason I think.*

It is always something outside us that upsets us and causes us pain, isn't it? Yet, when the pain is in us, how can we blame it on something outside? Why not simply see that we are upset? The lesson begins:

> *This idea... can be used with any person, situation or event you think is causing you pain.*

So, there are persons, situations, and events that are entertaining or pleasurable, and there are those that give us pain.

> *Apply it specifically to whatever you believe is the cause of your upset, using the description of the feeling in whatever term seems accurate to you.*

The *Course* says to apply this specifically. Have we ever been specific in our lives? We are vague and general, for the most part. Our casual minds are never factual or exact. To make inner correction, we have to come to precision.

Until you learn that form does not matter,
each form becomes a proper subject for the
exercises for the day. Applying the same idea
to each of them separately is the first step in
ultimately recognizing they are all the same.

You and I have the task of recognizing that these
feelings – anxiety, depression, jealousy, fear – are all
the same. Can we see that all of them do exactly the
same thing? They all upset us.

When using the idea for today for a specific
perceived cause of an upset in any form, use
both the name of the form in which you see
the upset, and the cause which you ascribe to
it. For example:

I am not angry at _____ for the reason I think.

Let's say I'm angry at Connie because she doesn't
do the accounting right. If I say to myself, "Never mind
Connie, I'll ask Sandi to do it," there is no correction.
My fear of loss and lack of trust are still in me. I'm
angry because I'm really afraid of loss.

I cannot keep this form of upset
and let the others go.

How unwilling we are to come to objective thought.
We value our upset over our peace of mind. Can we see
that whatever we think is a reaction? How do we come
to objective thought that is discriminate and precise?
To be factual is essential. When we are exact and

factual, we dissolve the casualness and lack of discrimination that causes our upset.

Why blame another? It is the ego that blames. The Holy Spirit sees only the holiness of God's creation.

The *Course* urges us repeatedly to call upon the Holy Spirit. Have we any intent to do so? The function of the Holy Spirit, whose thought is different from ours, is to correct us. But we are not interested in being corrected. We don't really want to step out of the pressure of our daily lives. We won't give the lesson five minutes. Could we realize that? That would be an amazing discovery.

> *Then search your mind for no more than a minute or so, and try to identify a number of different forms of upset that are disturbing you, regardless of the relative importance you may give them. Apply the idea for today to each of them, using the name of both the source of the upset as you perceive it, and of the feeling as you experience it. Further examples are:*
>
> *"I am not worried about _____ for the reason I think."*
> *"I am not depressed about _____ for the reason I think."*

Practice this. Just giving yourself the space helps you step out of the pressure you have imposed upon yourself. This lesson awakens the initiative to dispel illusions. You would never succumb to depression or self-indulgent upsets if you kept the pure spirit of this lesson alive.

Loss, attachment, resentment, and fear – aren't these all of our own making? It is not complicated or difficult; it is extremely simple. We are upset by our thoughts that do not mean anything.[5] We are upset because we live by thought, and the peace of God is of no importance to us. We are not determined to see.[6]

Do you value peace of mind? Is it of first importance to you? The only peace is the peace of God. There is no peace at the ego or personality level. And for us to be with the Will of God – with Absolute Knowledge – we have to bring our minds to that peace. But that is the one thing we avoid – coming to peace.

√ *I am never upset for the reason I think.*

√ This lesson introduces you to miracles that dissolve deception. The minute you see that you are never upset for the reason you think, a pure space untouched by thought is given you. You would value that purity so much that you would never go back to thought; you would always want to stay with that moment of eternity.

Then you would see how motives always distract you from it; how fear keeps you busy; how ambition and desire drive you. Can you see that motives never allow you to be who you really are?

Today is the day to use the energy and vibration of this lesson to end all upsets. To bring it into application will simplify your life.

One single day is all it takes. Once you have truly learned the lesson, you understand it forever because it is not of thought.

√Read the lesson lovingly. Free yourself from every upset. If you don't, how will you find the peace within you?

Exploring LESSON 6

"I am upset because I see something that is not there."*

If we are upset because we see something that is not there, we must be reacting to something we have projected. The upset is in *us*. Because it is in us, only we can deal with it.

All the reasons we give for our upset are not true because reasons are of the past. Whenever we go back to the past we see only that – the memory of some other person, event, or situation that we can blame. But there is no "other" in the present.

Can we die to yesterday? The action of each lesson of *A Course in Miracles* brings all the noises of yesterday to the present and silences them. We come to peace. The issue is always internal.

The exercises with this idea are very similar to the preceding ones. Again, it is necessary to name the form of upset (anger, fear, worry, depression and so on) and the perceived

---

* *A Course in Miracles, Workbook for Students*, page 10. [W-6. page 10.]

*source very specifically for any application
of the idea.*

The *Course* says to be specific. Can we experiment
and find out for ourselves how being specific and
factual gives us more energy? The power of precise
words is that they cannot be undone. Rather, they
dissolve both the past and the future. When we are really
precise, we are then capable of knowing something beyond
relative knowledge, beyond our likes and dislikes, beyond
the realm of our upsets.

Now we read,

> *For example, "I am angry at _____
> because I see something that is not there."*

What does the lesson mean by *For example...?* It
means that it is not enough to merely repeat the lesson
without doing the exercises. We have to find the time
to actually practice the lesson.

This is not so difficult, and yet we think it is. We
are so stimulated and busy with other things. Or we are
indifferent and lazy.

We are trying, with the help of the *Course*, to bring
the memory of God into our lives. When the remembrance of God is awakened in us, we become eternal.
Everything of time that attempts to distract us is taken
in and dissolved, and we are brought to purity. We can
then say to time, "You cannot regulate me. I am a
changed person."

Our real job is to find out what prevents us from doing the lesson in a very thorough way. This self-knowing need not make us helpless; it should awaken our confidence.

The lesson continues:

> *I am worried about _____ because I see something that is not there.*
>
> *Today's idea is useful for application to anything that seems to upset you, and can profitably be used throughout the day for that purpose.*

You may be saying, "What does the *Course* think, that I have nothing else to do today? I did the lesson in the morning, isn't that enough?" We don't have time for the lesson. Our anger, depression, and worry keep us busy. We are so reluctant to make inner correction that we don't even ask what correction is.

> *The three or four practice periods which are required should be preceded by a minute or so of mind searching, as before, in the application of the idea to each upsetting thought uncovered in the search.*

One minute of mind searching is a long time for a lazy person. We'd rather be shot in the leg. How resistant we are!

In practicing the lesson, we are trying to widen the gaps of silence between our thoughts. If we are anxious, the gaps of silence narrow and our thoughts crowd the space like a swarm of bees. But as we begin to relax, the silent gaps between our thoughts expand in a most natural way. It is possible to break thought's spell. Then our words become profound.

Let us discover the purity of space that is untouched by thought. One day there would be nothing that could take us away from it. We would simply go to thought, complete whatever thought had to do, and return to our "home base" – the recognition that we are eternal. Here on earth we do what needs to be done, but we return to Heaven to be at home.

Now the lesson says:

> *If you resist applying the idea to some upsetting thoughts more than others, remind yourself of the cautions stated in the previous lesson:*

> *There are no small upsets. They are all equally disturbing to my peace of mind.*

> *I cannot keep this form of upset and let the others go. For the purposes of these exercises, then, I will regard them all as the same.*

There are no small upsets.

Our brain exaggerates the irritation of an upset in the same way that we scratch an itch. Just seeing that we exaggerate and promote the upset is all we need to do. We do not have to suppress our feelings or know anything else. This awareness is an impersonal action.

Notice how the *Course* emphasizes peace of mind. We must look at everything that disturbs us and deprives us of peace. Unless we are at peace – which is our natural state – there will not be peace in the world. We are responsible for the continuing arms race, for war, for everything that is happening in the external world.

Instead of making causes and trying to change the world – and thereby adding to the tension and friction – why not come to peace ourselves? That is the only true action we can take. It is when we are frustrated, ambitious, or unfulfilled that we want to make causes. When you and I are at peace, we extend that peace to everything around us.

As long as we blind ourselves with projected upsets, we deny ourselves the vision of Reality. We must be determined to put an end to the past and come to newness.

The more space and leisure we give to our reading of the *Course,* the better chance we have of receiving its True Knowledge. Because we are creatures of habit, at first we resist. But we can determine to awaken an awareness in us which our body senses and habits cannot totally ignore. This is the beginning of honesty in life.

A Course in Miracles has come as a gift of God to His Son to awaken him from the *sleep of forgetfulness.* [7] If we are determined to awaken, we have the blessings and the Forces of the Universe behind us.

Exploring LESSON 7

"I see only the past."*

This should really hit you. Don't read further. Give yourself space.

I see only the past.

As you give it attention, you begin to recognize the truth of this. You discover, for instance, that you can't let go of what you think about a person, good or bad. So you can't see *him* or *her*.

Don't just keep reading. Find out if this is so. You will see that if you can't let go of your opinion about someone, *I see only the past* is a fact.

Now, we go into it a little deeper. We discover that when we see only the past, we don't see the present at all. How can we relate to the present if we are always in the past? Our knowing is of the past, our grievances are of the past, our gratefulness is of the past. How can we know what gratefulness is if we live in the past? So there is a lot to explore, isn't there? We are already

---

* *A Course in Miracles, Workbook for Students,* page 11. [W-7. page 11.]

challenged, and we have hardly begun to read the lesson.

Have you ever been in the present? Ask yourself. Can you recall a moment of danger – when you felt you would drown or be bitten by a rattlesnake? At that moment you were in the present, weren't you? When you were nearly run over, you had to move fast. Was it your learning from past experience or some other faculty that acted?

In danger you call upon an intelligence which is independent of the past. It is an instant action, swifter than thought, and unpredictable. You don't know what you are going to do.

One evening after dark, I was walking with a friend in Chandigarh, India. I stepped on a cobra. I leapt so high that only the cobra's hood struck my heel. That's how I was saved. Do you see how quick your reflexes are? You act! You're not going to wonder, "Did I step on a stick? Is this a rope?"

There is also an involuntary and creative action of Life within you which focuses your energy. To make contact with this creative action, you have to bring your brain to total stillness. In stillness, this energy can be concentrated wherever you direct it. Can you imagine what a joy it is to be that creative, to be totally in the present? You are so focused that the past doesn't touch you.

I see only the past.

You and I can discover this directly. As you become serious about the lesson, gradually the internal questioning begins. "How can I be in the past when I'm thinking about tomorrow?" But that is the past, too. It is the past that invented tomorrow. The fact is you do see only the past. You can't get out of it; it is like a tar pit. Even wanting to get out of it is the past.

You have to come to a burning vitality. You have to come to crisis.

I see only the past.

This idea is particularly difficult to believe at first. Yet it is the rationale for all of the preceding ones.

It is the reason why nothing you see means anything.

It is the reason why you have given everything you see all the meaning that it has for you.

It is the reason why you do not understand anything you see.

It is the reason why your thoughts do not mean anything, and why they are like the things you see.

Seeing only the past limits you. Conditioned and controlled by habit, you are not alive to the present. There is nothing new in what you do, today or ever in your life. Do you feel the agony of this predicament?

All the help of Heaven surrounds you if you are determined to bring today's lesson into application this very day.

I see only the past.

It is the reason why you are never upset for the reason you think.

It is the reason why you are upset because you see something that is not there.

Can you imagine that? You are upset because you see only the past. Are you, or anyone else, ever in the present? In the present, nobody ever does anything wrong. How can you punish another person? The reasons you think you have for being upset are past reasons.

Are we like animals? Animals, with their instincts, live in the past. Why do we human beings want to live in the past, when we can live in the present which is uncontaminated by the past? We don't want to step into the present because we're attached to our likes and dislikes, and we love our habits.

Old ideas about time are very difficult to change.

The *Course* says "very difficult." I have met two extensions of God in my life, and both of them said the same thing to me: "People seldom, if ever, change." So, in order to change, we really have to put our whole heart into it.

Old ideas about time are very difficult to change, because everything you believe is rooted in time...

If we really saw that our beliefs are rooted in time, it would disturb us so deeply, and make us so miserable, that we would burn to escape it. How can we read this lesson and not come to crisis? With our minds in the past, we will never know goodness, love, God, rightness, self-reliance, or gratefulness; we will never know the *Course.*

Now the lesson instructs us:

Look at a cup, for example. Do you see a cup, or are you merely reviewing your past experiences... What do you know about this cup except what you learned in the past? You would have no idea what this cup is, except for your past learning. Do you, then, really see it?

Give a pencil to an aborigine. He'd probably throw it away! Nothing from his past says it has value to him. He might show some interest in the soft thing at one end and the little metal band because he has never seen anything like them.

Why are we never lost in the wonder of things? Why don't we find the originality in ourselves to look at something in the present? Could we allow the rose to introduce us to wholeness, to the totality of all creation? The rose is not separate from the sun or the dew. In one instant it can introduce us to the vitality of the present.

In the present – in one split second – how many birds fly from one branch to another? How many fish dart from here to there? How many heartbeats pulse in that one second? What vitality!

We are happy in proportion to the attention we give something. I will cross the street just to see a rose. I saw a particularly beautiful saffron-colored rose growing at the bottom of a scrubby bush with a lot of thorns. It had an exquisite scent.

How extraordinary that the earth could produce such a rose. The beauty of the earth is expressed in flowers. How did they come into being? Who could imagine making soil from fallen leaves to nourish living things? It's a cycle that continues forever.

"I see only the past in this shoe."
"I see only the past in that body."

I give the body meaning in terms of what I know the body can do. For something to have real meaning, however, it has to be of Reality. Reality is beyond time; it doesn't change. So all these things – the pencil, the shoe, the body – have no meaning.

To be in the present, we have to let go of the past. Letting go has been our difficulty from the beginning of time. It is the only problem; there is no other. Being in the present is quite simple once we recognize that we see only the past. But we make it complicated. We say, "I have to think about it"; thus, we remain in the past.

✓ It is our responsibility to see that *we* continue the past, and that *we* have to end it. To know our own boundlessness, we must undo the past. No one can undo the past without the help of the Holy Spirit. When we discover that we need His help and call upon it, the action of the Holy Spirit ends the past and the future and brings us to the present.

Make sure you have the capacity to receive and to heed the Holy Spirit's help; otherwise, don't ask for it. You will lose faith and your asking will become a ritual. We usually ask for help without the capacity to receive; we do it merely as a duty. But underneath the duty there remains a deep yearning that brought us to the *Course* in the first place.

When you ask the Holy Spirit for help, be quiet for a while and see if you really mean it or if you are just convincing yourself. Make sure that you are attentive. Then find out if you were. If you were not, discover that you were dishonest.

Somewhere in each of us there is a yearning for a teacher. If you recognize the *Course,* you see it as the answer to your prayer. Now, when you ask for help, you have the capacity to receive. And you read it differently.

✓ We must come to passion to outgrow all that is rooted in time, for nothing of time has meaning. Once you realize the truth of this, you are a saint. And the earth is not the same with one saint upon it.

Exploring LESSON 8

"My mind is preoccupied with past thoughts."*

Does the title of this lesson make you pause? What happens when you read it? Do you think it is true? Not true? Does it make a difference either way? Isn't your agreement or disagreement just an idea?

When you agree or disagree with it as an idea, you discover that nothing happens to you. Do you see how irrelevant ideas are?

A miracle has happened if you've realized that ideas have no meaning.

When we remain at the level of ideas, no miracle takes place. We either condemn ourselves or become enthusiastic and say, "I'm really going to get this!" We feel guilty or pious. But both are reactions. Would it not be wiser to see that ideas don't fundamentally change us? Ideas are abstract. If you see this, then for a moment your mind is free of the past.

---

* *A Course in Miracles, Workbook for Students,* page 13. [W-8. page 13.]

No miracles take place when you condemn yourself: "Yes, I know I'm terrible." You may discover that you've been finding fault with yourself for years. But God created you. What right have you to find fault with yourself?

In the village in Punjab, India, where I was born, they say only a fool beats the calf when the cow doesn't give milk. That is how crazy your opinions of yourself are. Like all ideas, they are insane.

You go on to berate yourself: "I am supposed to see my perfection." This is also a mistake. As long as you generate ideas, you will continue to make mistakes. Do something about the *ideas* and leave yourself alone. When you question your ideas, you *are* as God created you. You are questioning the interpretations that have plagued humanity for centuries. This questioning effortlessly frees you from the authority of misperception – probably for the first time.

Do you see now that thought is the issue?

Ideas and thought are the same. Our minds are preoccupied with them. To apply this lesson would mean that whenever you become aware that your mind is preoccupied, you don't then analyze your thought or even try to do something about it. Awareness itself corrects you. You know that whatever preoccupies you blinds you and diverts your energy. It puts you back in the *sleep of forgetfulness*. Now, knowing that awareness is the means of correction, you are enriched for life.

If you are not vigilant, thought creeps in. The *Course* admits that. Your energy fluctuates; you become distracted or tired. But the minute the lesson comes to remembrance and you give it your attention and energy, a miracle undoes your thought. So, while the idea is there, the miracle is there also. The Given is accessible. The miracle's energy liberates you from preoccupation. You recognize that what absorbed you is no longer important.

You recognize further that as long as you are preoccupied, you are in the past, oblivious to the present.

> *The mind's preoccupation with the past is the cause of the misconception about time from which your seeing suffers. Your mind cannot grasp the present, which is the only time there is. It therefore cannot understand time, and cannot, in fact, understand anything.*

When you do the lesson, is your understanding just an idea or have you received a miracle? Do your questions reflect an interest in going deeper than understanding? Without that interest, your understanding is a preoccupation itself. You have to confront yourself and come to crisis.

The minute you put the lesson in second place, you choose to stay in the past. When you decide to "do it later," you've made your routine of first importance. Routines are for the survival of "me and mine." In your routine, you see nothing of the present. When you are self-centered, you deprive yourself of anything other than the images of your brain.

My mind is preoccupied with past thoughts.

Once you have understood this, you can catch yourself in the habit of thought. The miracle undoes your thought the instant you become aware. Soon you will love the awareness that renews your life more than the tiresome preoccupation of thought.

Awareness is effortless. It changes your values and liberates you from the past. Transformed, you are forever glad and grateful.

The human being extends the Will of God only when he is in the present, free from the illusion of time. The discovery of your own unwillingness to come to your Reality will lead you to challenge yourself. Seeing the fact as the fact is the miracle that imparts energy.

The one wholly true thought one can hold about the past is that it is not here. To think about it at all is therefore to think about illusions. Very few have realized what is actually entailed in picturing the past or in anticipating the future. The mind is actually blank when it does this, because it is not really thinking about anything.

While thoughtless ideas preoccupy your mind, the truth is blocked. Recognizing that your mind has been merely blank, rather than believing that it is filled with real ideas, is the first step to opening the way to vision.

Are not all problems of the past? We bring our past problems into the present; therefore, we never know the present which is impersonal, boundless, and vital. We know only problems. Mr. J. Krishnamurti said, "There are no problems apart from the mind."

If you were earnest, you would say, "I am always in the past. To awaken from this *sleep of forgetfulness,* I have to be attentive. But I can't be attentive. My mind is somewhere else. I am preoccupied all day long. There must be something meaningful to which I can give my attention. If I had an interest, then I would be with the present."

This discovery would bring you great happiness.

Interest and attention are essential first steps to bring you to a creative action where you can extend the Will of God.

If your interest is in something meaningful, you will awaken wisdom and the real abilities that you brought with you at birth to express. You will extend your God-nature upon the earth. Your interest and its energy will bring you to the present and to meaningful, intrinsic expression. You were born with a purpose and a function. You are a part of the One Awareness in which minds are joined.

We waste our energy with unessentials. Every day billions of lives and billions of tons of the earth's resources are used to make the meaningless. How can we contribute to this waste? What has happened to humanity – to each of us?

Is there anyone who listens anymore? Our pre-occupation with yesterday has become so self-destructive that there is no one with whom we can communicate our Oneness. Where there is "you and me" there is no communication. But do not personalize this or you will start to criticize someone else or condemn yourself. Genuine understanding is a springboard to something deeper.

Can you see the horror and the danger of being preoccupied all day with past thoughts and things that engage only your partial attention? Your "understanding" of this is only a concept. As an idea, it has no vitality. You are no different than before. Truly seeing this, however, awakens you to sanity.

Everything we do is a lie in the absence of total attention. Only what is eternal is Real. The *Course* is offering us the eternal words of True Knowledge, and we cannot hear them. To discover this would jolt us into responsibility. As long as we are irresponsible, we cannot know gratefulness or appreciation. If we lack interest, scriptures don't matter, real teachers don't matter. Nothing matters.

My mind is preoccupied with past thoughts.

This lesson blazes in the dark night of the world of separation. There is a light and a peace in reading just the title. We see that we have never stepped out of yesterday. Nor are we alive to the eternity of our own being – the light of creation. We are false to ourselves.

The wise person brings illusions to truth and dissolves them. He sees the false as the false. And then he sees that what he dislikes outside himself is what he is. He deals with himself, knowing his Reality cannot be threatened.

To realize the truth of today's lesson would change your life.

Exploring LESSON 9

"I see nothing as it is now."*

We look at everything through images of thought which keep the past alive. These images are not real because what is real is *right now*. Preoccupied with past thoughts, our minds breed endless illusions. We are not in the now. If we were in the now – this moment – we would not be able to name anything. When we isolate and name a flower, for example, we haven't seen it. When something is "seen" now, it relates us with eternity.

A flower could not *be* if, for millions of years, it had not rained, or if there were no air and sunlight. How many leaves went into making the soil around it. A flower can relate us to the very creation of this planet. It is a joyous expression of the eternal, creative force. It is not time-bound.

But we cannot experience wholeness in the present because we are caught in the past. What could be worse?

---

* *A Course in Miracles, Workbook for Students,* page 15. [W-9. page 15.]

√ How many centuries we have struggled without knowing this! At last we see that time is an illusion. Not chronological time, but psychological time – the illusion that *tomorrow* I am going to "get it."

So how do we change all our concepts? Just being honest about our illusions is helpful. True gratefulness is really the key. We do not have to *do* anything.

In this world, we struggle to get a degree and to make a living, so we think we have to struggle to become spiritual. Is it possible that our education has made us mediocre, that our efforts for self-survival are perverse? We are thrilled with our so-called achievements. But what value do achievements have if we don't know our boundlessness? We are here to bless the world, not settle for "wantings."

√ Everything that is of personality and time has struggle in it. True "seeing," or clarity, has no struggle in it because it dissolves the personality and frees us from time. It introduces us to our own eternity.

Every single lesson of the *Course* offers true seeing. One sentence starts the process, and by the end of the lesson, we can come to Atonement and serenity. When that does not take place, we have not read it.

√ The process starts by diminishing the brain's authority over us. When we think of the lesson in the midst of our daily lives, we free ourselves from the pressures of time. We become truly sensitive and appreciative. Then the only art is the art of living.

I see nothing as it is now.

*This idea obviously follows
from the two preceding ones:*

I see only the past
and
My mind is preoccupied with past thoughts.

Have we really grasped these lessons? We should be evolving with every lesson in a daily process of undoing. The *Course* is a joyous adventure.

I see nothing as it is now.

While you may be able to accept it intellectually, it is unlikely that it will mean anything to you as yet. However, understanding is not necessary at this point. In fact, the recognition that you do not understand is a prerequisite for undoing your false ideas. These exercises are concerned with practice, not with understanding.

If we just learn the lesson intellectually, we are not transformed by it. It's just like school – we learn from books and repeat what we learned on an exam. Mere memorization never goes past the brain.

Self-knowing is not intellectual. We will never know who we are as long as we defend intellectuality and dishonesty. To recognize this could transform our lives! Unfortunately, instead of coming to honesty, we become evasive. We justify our actions or we become confused.

V Can we see that we intellectualize our behavior? For example, if we say we are going to call a friend and then do not, we offer justifications for not doing so. We don't see the fact that we don't care.

V Every incident is a mirror in which we can see ourselves. If we do not want to uncover our isolation, selfishness, and reactions, then we are not serious. And to undo them, we must see things as they are. Correction does not take place otherwise. We deny the gift of the lesson and waste opportunities for undoing when we rely on intellectuality.

V Can we undo the pretense of intellectuality? We must train our minds to see the falseness of our assumptions and conclusions. The mind can be trained to be so incorruptible, so vigilant, that nothing of the past can intrude.

The *Course* says understanding is not necessary at this point. Our current level of understanding is just intellectual, so don't bother with it. Instead, the *Course* emphasizes practice. It says, in effect, "Practice is the doorway. Go through it, not through the window."

Then what is entailed in practicing the lesson?

You do not need to practice what you already understand. It would indeed be circular to aim at understanding, and assume that you have it already.

It is difficult for the untrained mind to believe that what it seems to picture is not there. This idea can be quite disturbing, and may meet

with active resistance in any number of forms.
Yet that does not preclude applying it.

The lesson says that because our minds are not trained, practice is necessary. So, practice must have something to do with training the mind. Is *our* practice, though, merely a form of activity? Even admitting that it is would be deceptive if that admission is only intellectual. Seeing this, in itself, is the action. A miracle has taken place the minute you question intellectuality and see it. You are no longer the same person. It just requires honesty to see our deceptions.

A mind that is trained to step out of thought – even for a split second – declares the existence of awareness. Thought has no power in the presence of awareness. If we put our whole heart into our practice, the awakening process begins. But partial attention won't work. It is self-deceptive.

Life is stronger than personality. Why do we endow personality with such power? We can step out of our bondage to it and be grateful. Then we become creative – the old dies and the new *is*.

Each small step will clear a little of the darkness away, and understanding will finally come to lighten every corner of the mind that has been cleared of the debris that darkens it.

Awareness is not intellectual; it undoes all that is born of thought and fear. Just our seeing ends activity. Self-honesty is the light. We have no other responsibility

than to be honest to ourselves. Then we are a blessing
upon the earth.

Exploring LESSON 10

"My thoughts do not mean anything."*

The space we give anything we read determines its impact on us. If we read the lesson hurriedly, it's just a lot of words. You see, our minds are always preoccupied. That's a fact.

When we approach something sacred, we need to do our part in making that space by sitting quiet for a while first.

The *Course* urges us to read slowly, that is, with attention. Attention asks: What does this mean? What am I being asked to see? The *Course* asks us to work with the lesson precisely, objectively. Do we know what that means? Are we ever precise? If we made these demands of ourselves, we would be responsible and wise. We would no longer be vague, indifferent, or casual. Each lesson offers a challenge which our inherent unwillingness wants to evade. *My thoughts do not mean anything* is quite a challenge.

---

* *A Course in Miracles, Workbook for Students,* page 16. [W-10. page 16.]

179

If *my thoughts do not mean anything,* then why am I so sure of them? Why do I assert myself? Why do I defend my position? If *my thoughts do not mean anything,* can I judge another? Ask yourself. Stay with it.

The first paragraph contains the gist of the lesson.

> *This idea applies to all the thoughts*
> *of which you are aware....*

Now what happens? You either see the truth of this, ignore it, or disagree. Which one is it? Do you ignore it? How are you going to find out if you are ignoring it? Isn't that thought also?

> *This idea applies to all the thoughts of which*
> *you are aware, or become aware in the*
> *practice period.*

The practice period demands that you actively participate, that you become aware of the fleeting thoughts that cross your mind.

> *The reason the idea is applicable to all of*
> *them is that they are not your real thoughts.*

Not your real thoughts? Are you making the thoughts you are thinking now real?

Can you begin to question your thoughts about yourself, people you know, things that happen?

It's very difficult to admit that you don't know — you don't know yourself or anyone else. Humility alone could admit that. Humility is a precious gift that is given you when you realize your thoughts do not mean anything.

My thoughts do not mean anything.

The reason the idea is applicable to all of them is that they are not your real thoughts. We have made this distinction before, and will do so again. You have no basis for comparison as yet.

Could you stop and see what comparison means?

At the level of unreality, all you see are differences between this and that. And this duality is both inside and outside of you. It is the source of the painful and utterly unessential conflict in your life. From the perspective of Reality, however, these differences are immaterial.

Discrimination can distinguish real thought from meaningless thought and thereby end conflict. Meaningless thoughts are always in conflict. You like somebody one moment and the next moment you don't. Over one little thing you change your mind about that person, and then your feelings are hurt. Thought is the mother of feeling. You think your feelings are always real whether thought is or not.

You have no basis for comparison as yet. When you do, you will have no doubt that what you once believed were your thoughts did not mean anything.

Let me ask you, "What happens when you realize that your thoughts do not mean anything?" If it is not your actual experience, you will still entertain meaningless thoughts. If it is your actual experience, you will say, "I become aware." And I would ask you, "What do you become aware of?" You might respond, *"My thoughts do not mean anything."*

However, if you are truly aware, you see that your thoughts are based on fear, insecurity, and loneliness. Your awareness introduces you to your fear. Then, for a moment, the same awareness shifts your state of being from fear to love.

Only when you put energy into it does this shift take place. You see in a fundamental way that your thoughts are based on fear. That is why they do not mean anything. But there are also real thoughts – thoughts of love.

You may think you've grasped the difference between meaningless thought and real thought, but are you just replacing one thought with another? Can you see that your thinking is still meaningless? You simply have a new idea. See how you fool yourself in thinking you've learned something new. When you give it meaning, meaningless thought poses as real.

Do you see that the thought in which you believe prevents you from realizing your real thought? If you do, then the real thought, which you didn't know before, releases and liberates you.

The *Course* says,

You have no basis for comparison as yet. When you do, you will have no doubt that what you once believed were your thoughts did not mean anything.

The shift has taken place from relying on your thought to receiving the help that real thought offers.

Does your heart leap with joy that something you never knew before would help you come to awareness? That is the boon of the lesson. It is not a teaching; it is a different energy. It is the energy of Heaven helping you. Have you received that gift? Would you insist upon having space to receive it?

The exercises consist, as before, in searching your mind for all the thoughts that are available to you, without selection or judgment. Try to avoid classification of any kind. In fact, if you find it helpful to do so, you might imagine that you are watching an oddly assorted procession going by, which has little if any personal meaning to you. As each one crosses your mind, say:

"My thought about _____
does not mean anything."

We have no quarrel with the birds, the trees, or the flowing river. Our only difficulty is with people.

There is always someone you are thoroughly, fanatically convinced has wronged you. Years pass by and your memory of that offense never loses its power.

And when the *Course* asks you to think of someone you really dislike, one name instantly comes to mind. Would you say that your thoughts about that person are meaningless?

Could this be the lesson which heals that grievance? Would you be willing to dissolve your dislike? Could you give the issue some space, so that you are released from the pain of it?

Close your eyes. Sit quietly and remember the person you think has deceived or harmed you. Think about that person. Notice that he or she is not present. Discover that it is only your opinion that he or she is bad. See if you can allow yourself to receive the help the lesson promises. What would take place then?

Let me put it another way. You are asking the Holy Spirit to help you be free of your grievance. Now you need to find out whether your prayer is real or just an idea.

Start to discover the way your mind works. Is it just your idea that you want to be released or is it your real intent? Perhaps you discover you don't want to be released. What is it that you really don't want? My explanation of this takes time, but your actual experience of it can be instantaneous. You can know whether or not you really want to be released.

What is the difference between accepting help and convincing yourself that you have forgiven another? If you believe you have forgiven that person without the help of Heaven, you are mistaken. Your "forgiveness" is just a meaningless belief.

But if you have accepted help, the difference is obvious. Your love immediately goes out to that person. Immediately. You would see that they misperceived just as you misperceived. There is no longer guilt in your mind; nor do you see the other person as guilty. The past ends. You look kindly toward that person. And your release is not a belief. You've received help, and the help is the love you give.

Forgiveness offers you everything you want. [8] And there is nothing your forgiveness cannot do. If you have forgiven one person, you can receive help to forgive another. But you will never take the credit yourself – that *you* did it. You will be grateful that the love of God flows through you.

*   *   *

I want you to know one thing. Just the blessing of your contact with *A Course in Miracles* can totally transform your views. Don't conclude that you can't change; you've already changed. You will never be the same. Why not be grateful?

Your gratefulness would show you a positive and sane view of life. It would even hasten your ascent up the spiral. Once you have made contact with the action of Life behind appearances, you would start undoing everything that blocks it.

You don't have to believe in anything. Just be responsible for undoing your own negativity. If you undermine yourself, you'll never trust. Once you have the *Course,* you can afford to trust.

As I have said, we must have yearned for thousands of years for truth. Religious organizations tend to degenerate into business or belief systems. They don't really care for you. So God had to take direct action to reach His Son. Now the *Course* is in your hands. Could you be inspired by this?

The minute you've made contact with the *Course,* it is impossible for you not to change. See the fact as the fact and start to undo. For that, you have all the help you can accept.

"This is my holy instant of release."

"Father, it is today that I am free, because my will is Yours. I thought to make another will. Yet nothing that I thought apart from You exists. And I am free because I was mistaken, and did not affect my own reality at all by my illusions. Now I give them up, and lay them down before the feet of truth, to be removed forever from my mind. This is my holy instant of release. Father, I know my will is one with Yours."

And so today we find our glad return to Heaven, which we never really left. The Son of God this day lays down his dreams. The Son of God this day comes home again, released from sin and clad in holiness, with his right mind restored to him at last.

Lesson 227
A Course in Miracles

OUR COMMON GOAL

Ours is a common task. Each one is called,
And he will answer as he makes the choice
To give up madness, and to choose instead
To recognize and to accept God's Voice.
Each one will waken at the time and place
That he has chosen, and will take his part
In the Atonement's purpose. For he came
With resurrection's calling in his heart.
He must attain a glorious rebirth,
And scatter stars across the sleeping earth.*

* This poem is from *The Gifts of God* (©1982, Foundation for Inner Peace) by Helen
Schucman, the Scribe of *A Course in Miracles*, page 35. It is an incomparable book of
poetry containing some of the most important words ever written.

APPENDICES

The Purpose of the
Foundation for Life Action

The Purpose of the Foundation for Life Action
is to be with the Eternal Laws
so that it does not become an organization.

LOVE IS ETERNAL.
ABILITIES EXTENDING LOVE ARE BLESSED.

In the absence of Love
abilities become the bondage of skills,
limited to personality.
Among virtuous men,
it is what the human being IS that is Real,
and not what he does in a body.

The Purpose of the Foundation is to be part of

GOD'S PLAN FOR SALVATION. [1]

Thus it has a different point of reference
than the thought system of man.

Obviously, the Name of God
cannot be commercialized.
There are no fees in what we share.
We do not believe in loss and gain.

Non-commercial action is provided by
the blessings of productive life.

"In God we trust."

Those who are with the Eternal Laws
in times of change remain unaffected.
In crisis, it is your care for another
that is your strength.

We have a function in the world
to be truly helpful to others,
knowing:

I am sustained by the love of God. [2]

My only function is the one God gave me. [3]

Nothing real can be threatened.
Nothing unreal exists. [4]

We are not pressured by the brutality of success.
We are blessed by the work we do.
Gratefulness is complete, as love is independent.

To us, you, the human being, comes first.
Thus it enables us to go past
the conventional opinion of right and wrong
and relate directly to you.

For man is as God created him,
unchanged by the changeable society
that rules his body with its belief systems.

The Truth is a Fact that dissolves illusions of time.
Our function is to dispel the abstraction of ideas
and realize the actuality of Fact.
For,

I am under no laws but God's. [5]

Reverence for Life is of a still mind
hallowed by His Love.
This transformation is what we call

THE PATH OF VIRTUE.

The Path of Virtue is the ministry of gratefulness.
The wise who extends
the Kingdom of God on earth
lives consistent with

"BUT SEEK YE FIRST
THE KINGDOM OF GOD,
AND HIS RIGHTEOUSNESS;
AND ALL THINGS
SHALL BE ADDED UNTO YOU." [6]

Biography of Tara Singh

Tara Singh is known as a teacher, author, poet, and humanitarian. The early years of his life were spent in a small village in Punjab, India. From this sheltered environment, at the age of nine, he and his mother and sisters traveled to Panama via Europe to join his father who was in business there. While in Panama he attended school for two years. At the age of eighteen, he returned to India. At twenty-two, inspired by the family saint, his search for Truth led him to the Himalayas where he lived for four years as an ascetic. During his period he outgrew conventional religion. He discovered that a mind conditioned by religious or secular beliefs is always limited.

In his next phase of growth, he responded to the poverty of India through participation in that country's postwar industrialization and international affairs. He became an associate of Mahatma Gandhi, and a close friend not only of Prime Minister Nehru, but also of Eleanor Roosevelt.

It was in the 1950's, as he outgrew his involvement with political and economic systems, that Mr. Singh was inspired by his association with Mr. J. Krishnamurti and the teacher of the Dalai Lama. He discovered that humanity's problems cannot be solved externally. Subsequently, he became more and more removed from worldly affairs and devoted several years of his life to the study and practice of yoga. The discipline imparted through yoga helped make possible a three year period of silent retreat in Carmel, California, in the early 1970's.

As he emerged from the years of silence in 1976, he came into contact with *A Course in Miracles*. Its impact on him was profound. He recognized its unique contribution as a scripture and saw it as the answer to man's urgent need for direct contact with Truth. There followed a close relationship with its Scribe. The *Course* has been the focal point of his life ever since. Mr. Singh recognizes and presents the *Course* as the Thoughts of God, and correlates it with the great spiritual teachings and religions of the world.

From Easter 1983 to Easter 1984, Mr. Singh conducted the One Year Non-Commercialized Retreat: A Serious Study of *A Course in Miracles*. It was an unprecedented, in-depth exploration of the *Course*. No tuition was charged. Since then, Mr. Singh has worked on a one-to-one basis with a small group of serious students under the sponsorship of the Foundation for Life Action.

Tara Singh is the author of numerous books, audiotapes, and videotapes in which he discusses the action of bringing one's life into order, freeing oneself from past conditioning, living the principles of *A Course in Miracles,* and coming to inner awakening. Mr. Singh offers an annual week-long retreat at Easter for those wishing to make a sustained contact with him.

REFERENCES

References are cited for the first edition of *A Course in Miracles,* ©1975, followed in brackets by the corresponding book, chapter, section, paragraph, sentence, and page for the second edition, ©1992, of the *Course.* For example, the citation [T-16. III. 4;1. page 335.] refers to *Text,* Chapter 16, Section III, paragraph 4, sentence 1, page 335.

PREFACE

1. *A Course in Miracles* (ACIM), first published in 1976 by the Foundation for Inner Peace, Glen Ellen, California, is a contemporary scripture that deals with the psychological/spiritual issues which face all humanity. It consists of three volumes: *Text* (I) [T], *Workbook for Students* (II) [W], and *Manual for Teachers* (III) [M]. The *Text,* 669 pages, sets forth the concepts on which the thought system of the *Course* is based. The *Workbook for Students,* 488 pages, is designed to make possible the application of the concepts presented in the *Text* and consists of three hundred and sixty-five lessons, one for each day of the year. The *Manual for Teachers,* 92 pages, provides answers to some of the basic questions a student of the *Course* might ask and defines many of the terms used in the *Text.* Editor
2. ACIM, III, page 25. [M-9. 2;1-2. page 26.]
3. ACIM, I, page 312. [T-16. III. 4;1. page 335.]
4. ACIM, I, page 313. [T-16. III. 8;1. page 336.]
5. ACIM, II, page 18. [W-11. page 18.]
6. ACIM, II, page 48. [W-31. page 48.]
7. ACIM, II, page 239. [W-133. page 245.]
8. ACIM, III, page 67. [M-29. 2;6-10. page 70.]
9. ACIM, III, page 68. [M-29. 5;9. page 71.]
10. ACIM, III, page 1. [M-introduction. 1;5. page 1.]
11. ACIM, III, page 5. [M-2. 5;5. page 6.]
12. ACIM, II, page 219. [W-124. 12;2. page 224.]
13. ACIM, I, page 6. [T-1. III. 1;1-6. page 8.]
14. Ibid.
15. ACIM, I, page 444. [T-22. IV. page 477.]
16. Refers to Matthew 13:13-17.

202 / A GIFT FOR ALL MANKIND

17. ACIM, I, page 444. [T-22. IV. 1;1-7. page 477.]
18. See ACIM, I, pages 426-427; II, page 120 and following. [T-21. V. 5, 6, 7. pages 457-458. W-71. page 121.]
19. Refers to the *Purpose of the Foundation* written by Tara Singh February 27, 1982. See Appendix, page 193.
20. ACIM, III, page 8. [M-4. I. 1;4-7. page 9.]
21. ACIM, II, page 89. [W-55. 4(24);1-3. page 91.]
22. ACIM, II, page 120. [W-71. page 121.]
23. ACIM, II, page 107. [W-65. page 108.]
24. ACIM, II, page 434. [W-292. page 444.]
25. ACIM, II, page 233. [W-131. page 239.]

CHAPTER ONE: WHY *A COURSE IN MIRACLES?*

1. Refers to John 10:30.
2. ACIM, II, page 79. [W-50. page 79.]
3. John 14:12.
4. ACIM, II, page 3. [W-1. page 3.]
5. ACIM, II, page 4. [W-2. page 4.]
6. ACIM, II, page 6. [W-4. page 6.]
7. ACIM, II, page 16. [W-10. page 16.]
8. ACIM, II, page 77. [W-48. page 77.]
9. ACIM, II, page 79. [W-50. page 79.]
10. Exodus 20:13.
11. "In God We Trust" appears to have been inspired by a line from *The Star Spangled Banner,* "In God is our trust," written by Francis Scott Key in 1814. "In God We Trust" first appeared on the coinage of the United States in 1864, during the presidency of Abraham Lincoln. It became the official motto of the United States in 1956. – Editor
12. ACIM, II, page 119. [W-70. 9;3-4. page 120.]
13. ACIM, I, introduction. [T-introduction. page 1.]
14. ACIM, II, page 392. [W-221. page 402.]
15. Ibid.

CHAPTER TWO: APPROACHING TRUTH – HOW TO READ *A COURSE IN MIRACLES*

1. ACIM, II, page 406. [W-245.1;1-8; and 2;1-3. page 416.]
2. ACIM, II, page 437. [W-298. page 447.]
3. ACIM, II, page 18. [W-11. page 18.]
4. ACIM, II, page 51. [W-34. page 51.]
5. ACIM, II, page 18. [W-11. page 18.]

6. ACIM, II, page 16. [W-10. page 16.]
7. ACIM, II, page 119. [W-70. 9;3-4. page 120.]
8. John 16:33.

CHAPTER THREE: THE CHALLENGE OF LIVING *A COURSE IN MIRACLES*

1. ACIM, II, page 290. [W-157. 9;1-3. page 297.]
2. John 13:34; 15:12-17.
3. ACIM, II, page 239. [W-133. page 245.]
4. ACIM, II, page 79. [W-50. page 79.]
5. ACIM, II, page 476. [W-361. page 486.]
6. ACIM, I, introduction. [T-introduction. 2;2-3. page 1.]
7. Refers to *I am sustained by the love of God,* Lesson 50 of *A Course in Miracles.* See ACIM, II, page 79. [W-50. page 79.]
8. ACIM, I, page 6. [T-1. III. 1;1. page 8]
9. ACIM, II, page 192. [W-108. 8; 6-8. page 196.]
10. Ibid.

CHAPTER FOUR: THE DAILY LESSON OFFERS MIRACLES

1. ACIM, I, page 326. [T-16. VII. 12;4. page 350.]
2. ACIM, III, page 62. [M-26. 4;8. page 65.]
3. ACIM, II, page 471. [W-354. page 481.]
4. Refers to *Truth will correct all errors in my mind,* Lesson 107 of *A Course in Miracles.* See ACIM, II, page 189. [W-107. page 192.]
5. Refers to *These thoughts do not mean anything. They are like the things I see in this room [on this street, from this window, in this place],* Lesson 4 of *A Course in Miracles.* See ACIM, II, page 6. [W-4. page 6.]
6. Refers to *I am determined to see,* Lesson 20 of *A Course in Miracles.* See ACIM, II, page 31. [W-20. page 31.]
7. ACIM, I, page 326. [T-16. VII. 12;4. page 350.]
8. Refers to *Forgiveness offers everything I want,* Lesson 122 of *A Course in Miracles.* See ACIM, II, page 213. [W-122. page 217.]

THE PURPOSE OF THE FOUNDATION FOR LIFE ACTION

1. See ACIM, I, page 426-427; II, page 120 and following. [T-21. V. 5,6,7. page 457; W-71. page 121.]
2. ACIM, II, page 79. [W-50. page 79.]
3. ACIM, II, page 107. [W-65. page 108.]
4. ACIM I, introduction. [T-introduction. 2;2-3. page 1.]
5. ACIM, II, page 132. [W-76. page 134.]
6. Matthew 6:33.

Other Materials by Tara Singh Related To *A Course in Miracles*

BOOKS

The Future of Mankind –
    Affluence without Wisdom Is Self-Destructive
Awakening a Child from Within
Commentaries on A Course in Miracles
How to Learn from A Course in Miracles
"Nothing Real Can Be Threatened"
Dialogues on A Course in Miracles
How to Raise a Child of God
"Love Holds No Grievances" – The Ending of Attack
Jesus and the Blind Man – Commentaries on St. John, Chapter IX
The Present Heals
Remembering God in Everything You See
Moment Outside of Time
The Joseph Plan of A Course in Miracles for the Lean Years

AUDIOCASSETTES

Service – Finding Something of Your Own to Give
Keep the Bowl Empty
Awakening the Light of the Mind
True Meditation – A Practical Approach
In God We Trust
Conflict Ends with Me
What Is A Course In Miracles?
A Course In Miracles Explorations
"What Is the Christ?"
"Creation's Gentleness Is All I See"
Undoing Self-Deception
All Relationships Must End in Love
Is It Possible to Rest the Brain?

Discovering Your Life's Work
The Heart of Forgiveness

AUDIO CASSETTE COLLECTIONS

The Foundation For Life Action makes it possible for individuals to access the wisdom from the sharings given by Tara Singh over the nine years with his students. The following audio tape series provide a profound experience for the serious student, whether or not he/she is studying A Course In Miracles.

THE ONE YEAR NON-COMMERCIALIZED RETREAT:
A SERIOUS STUDY OF A COURSE IN MIRACLES.

72 ninety-minute audio cassette tapes covering the most essential talks given by Mr. Singh during the One Year Non-Commercialized Retreat: A Serious Study of A Course In Miracles. *Includes sharings on the Text and Lessons of the Course, Creation, Yoga, Holy Beings, Silence, Integrity, Forgiveness and many, many other topics.*

THE FLOWERING OF WISDOM

A carefully selected series of fifty tapes which includes the most significant talks with students by Mr. Singh over the eight years following the One Year Retreat in 1983. These sharings are selected to give serious students an opportunity for growth as they deepen their understanding of A Course In Miracles, *relationships and their life's purpose. Included in this series are tapes on:*
Living a Life Without Preferences
Making Contact with the Holy Spirit
Developing the Capacity to Receive
Discovering One's Own Ordained Work of the Day
Laws of Transformation
Man-Woman Relationships

"As I listened to these tapes, there was a deep stirring within and a sense of great silence. Only after the tape had finished did I recognize that my brain and thoughts were still. This must be the 'gaps between the thoughts' that Tara Singh speaks of, and up until now, had not been my direct experience. Indeed these sharings are timeless and immense."
S.S., New Zealand

HOLDING HANDS WITH YOU –
EXPLORING THE DAILY LESSON OF THE COURSE

This new 25 tape series is made exclusively from Tara Singh's sharings on A Course In Miracles Workbook Lessons 1 to 50. Tara Singh shares profound insight, introducing the listener to key steps that will enable him or her to make his own discoveries about the lessons. They can shed a new light that brings you to the state of being that the lesson was intended to impart.

MANUAL FOR TEACHERS

This ten tape collection is a must for dedicated students of A Course In Miracles. Mr. Singh brings clarity to this very important volume of the Course through his insightful wisdom and tremendous background.

VIDEOCASSETTES

"There Must Be Another Way"
The Power of Attention
How to Raise a Child of God
A Course in Miracles Is Not to Be Learned, but to Be Lived

Book and tape catalogue
is available upon request from:
LIFE ACTION PRESS
P.O. Box 48932
Los Angeles, California 90048
800/367-2246
213/964-5444

Retreats and Workshops

ANNUAL EASTER RETREAT WITH TARA SINGH

Once each year Tara Singh meets for a week-long retreat with those of serious intent to share his wisdom on A Course In Miracles. *The location and date vary from year to year.*

NATIONWIDE RETREATS
WITH STUDENTS OF TARA SINGH

Join veteran speakers who have given their lives to living A Course in Miracles *for a weekend retreat of exploration. Bring your questions about the* Course *or your life to students who are studying with Tara Singh. You will also explore healing relationships, discovering your Life's purpose, having something to give to another, keys to stepping out of pressure, and deepening your inner growth. For more information, contact the Foundation for Life Action at 213-933-5591.*